FIRESIDE

Books by Mary Summer Rain

Nonfiction

Spirit Song
Phoenix Rising
Dreamwalker
Phantoms Afoot
Earthway
Daybreak
Soul Sounds
Whispered Wisdom
Ancient Echoes
Bittersweet
Mary Summer Rain's Guide to Dream Symbols
The Visitation
Millennium Memories
Fireside

Fiction

The Seventh Mesa

Children's

Mountains, Meadows and Moonbeams
Star Babies

Books on Tape

Spirit Song
Phoenix Rising
Dreamwalker
Phantoms Afoot
The Visitation

FIRESIDE

Mary Summer Rain

Cover design by Jane Hagaman
Cover photo by Grace Pedalino,
taken courtesy of Boar's Head Inn,
Charlottesville, Virginia

For information write:

Hampton Roads Publishing Company, Inc.
134 Burgess Lane
Charlottesville, VA 22902

Or call: (804) 296-2772
FAX: (804) 296-5096
e-mail: hrpc@hrpub.com
Website: www.hrpub.com

If you are unable to order this book from your local bookseller, you may order directly from the publisher. Quantity discounts for organizations are available. Call 1-800-766-8009, toll-free.

Library of Congress Cataloging in Publication Number: 98-71579

ISBN 1-57174-094-5

10 9 8 7 6 5 4 3 2 1

Printed on acid-free paper in Canada

FIRESIDE

FOREWORD

Have you ever spent a companionable evening at a friend's house where the mellow atmosphere made you comfortable enough to talk about whatever came to mind? Where subject matters ranging from the personal to the profound were touched upon and sparked to life like a dancing firefly on a midsummer night? Experiencing an evening of conversation that's relaxed and open enough to have no taboo issues and is rich in honest, straightforward expressions of warmth fills one's heart.

It is for these reasons that I have extended a friendly invitation for you to share such an evening with me. On this crisp autumn night I invite my readers to sit by the snapping woodstove fire and allow the grounding fragrance of burning cedar to encircle your beingness while you listen in on just one of the many eclectic conversations that, until now, were only heard by the receiving essence of my cabin's benevolent soul.

It was late September and the Autumn Spirit was more resplendent than I'd ever seen her. A profusion of ruby garnets adorned her spectacular gown this year. The golden and bright orange mountainsides surrounding my cabin were highlighted by the brilliant gemstone reds that sparkled and flared when touched by the gentle breeze; a breeze that whispered a fresh and crisp new breath so high up at ten thousand feet.

At seven o'clock in the morning, as was my routine, I lounged in the well-worn reading chair by the front window. Comfy in my robe and listening to the crackling woodstove, I was content with coffee cup in hand and watching the flocks of rosy finches feeding on the covered porch. Along with the finches, two kinds of chickadees were there, as well as Mr. and Mrs. Woodpecker. A lone Clark's nutcracker, as usual, made his own bid for the sunflower seeds.

I eagerly watched for the appearance of the pretty pine grosbeak, whose cheery voice always brought a smile to my heart. There's something truly joyous about birdsong.

Although this newly acquired cabin was remote, the thousands of birds, some squirrels, rabbits, and countless chipmunks who came to dine on my porch made me feel that I always had company around.

As I now watched the flurry of activity, my attention was sparked by the sudden disappearance of the four-leggeds. The mad dash marking their mass exit flustered the smaller birds into quickly seeking shelter within the blue branches of the porchside spruce. Only the brave finches continued to eat undisturbed.

A newcomer had arrived.

Perched atop the radiant orange aspen that grew tall beside the spruce was the valley's resident redtail hawk. Oh, this was no ordinary redtail. This one was so big that I had thought it was an owl the first time I'd seen it, for it'd had its feathers fluffed out in protection against one autumn morning's chill. At the time, I'd been so sure it was an owl that I grabbed the binoculars from the chairside table to get a closer look at it; however, the long red tail was what gave away its true identity. Since then, the hawk would frequently come to rest atop that same aspen, sit a spell while looking around, then gracefully fly off. Oh, he was truly a magnificent being and I felt fully blessed to count him as one of the visitors whose presence graced my simple abode.

Now I secretly watched him for a bit before I spoke to my friend, who was sitting across the room with her own morning's wake-up cup of steaming brew.

Then, "Sally, the hawk's back," I whispered.

Immediately she crossed the room to peer out the window. She knew right where to look.

My friend loved birds, so much so that she'd watch a soaring hawk or eagle while driving. That unnerved me the first time it happened. But now she grinned wide at me and sat on the cedar chest beneath the window to *observe* our beautiful visitor. As she watched him, I watched and listened to her as she expressed heartfelt joy while making eye contact with the grand bird just beyond the window. Her childlike wonder made my own heart smile. I wondered where I'd be without this completely selfless person who'd been sent to see me through some rough times. Her supportive help and companionship had been priceless.

"Oh! Look at him soar down through the valley!" she exclaimed while turning a beaming face to me. "I love it when he comes!" Then, as she went to refresh her coffee, I was left with an inner smile while returning my gaze out the window.

The pine grosbeak chirped its merry song while it munched on the seed piled high in the squirrel feeder.

I sighed. Life was so different now, so tranquil, so . . . good.

My friend appeared beside my chair. Steaming percolator in hand, she pointed to my empty cup.

I handed it over and thanked her for the refill.

Upon returning to the living room, Sally settled back into her usual place on the love seat.

We sat in silence for a while as we watched the busy porch activity or the little Yorkies comically romp around together on the carpet. So often the little furry ones brought the sound of my own laughter to my ears. There were four of them. Baby was Sally's Yorkie and the mother of my three: Pinecone, Rosebud, and Punkin Pie. My keeshond, Cheyenne, had watched their birth when we were still living in my three-room stone cabin. We still joke about that event to this day because, although Baby had birthed three pups, we were sure there was one more yet to be born. My daughter, Jenny, and her husband, Bill, were over at the time and Bill too thought one more pup was left in Baby. Feeling a lump of hardness in Baby's belly, I urged her to contract more. Poor Baby pushed and labored. She tried so hard. Turns out it was her uterus I was trying to birth! I don't think I'd make a great midwife. So this second litter produced two females and a male. I kept the two females and named them Rosebud and Punkin Pie. The little male went to a deputy sheriff friend of mine who also has ferrets running around his house. Pinecone was from Baby's first litter.

Now, as we sipped our coffee and watched the antics of the little ones, Sally commented that we were getting low on some of our staple supplies. "We need to restock," she said.

I withheld a groan. Restocking meant a trip down to Colorado Springs—a trip I never looked forward to.

"We could put it off for a few more days, but some items are getting critical," she added, knowing how much I didn't want to go.

"Mmmm, I know. I went to use the bathroom cleaner yesterday and I finished the little that was left."

Neither of us said more. It was almost as if we were delaying the decision for a few more prolonged moments.

She offered a solution. "If you want, we can work on a list and I can go do it."

"No," I said, "it's time for me to sign books again. I really need to do that. It's been a while."

Our city trips averaged one every ten weeks or so and, while downtown, I'd stop in certain bookstores to sign their stock of my titles. The owners and managers of these stores liked that, especially when they kept good stock. I appreciated their diligent attention and it was my way of showing gratitude.

So my restful wake-up time came to an abrupt end while we made our list of needed staples and got ready to leave the cabin for the day.

"Want to drive this time?" Sally asked as we walked out the gate to her '87 Corolla.

I shot her an incredulous look and rolled my eyes. "Even if I owned a car of my own, you'd be appointed the designated driver. Nope, no thanks, traffic's too crazy downtown for me. You can do the honors."

"You sure?" she checked.

I answered by comfortably settling myself into the passenger seat and mumbling.

"What?" she asked while turning the engine over.

"Nothing," I smiled.

Grinning back at me, "What'd you say?"

"I was just hoping no hawks would have your sights on the sky instead of on the road today."

"I can manage both," she defended, shoving the stick in reverse. "I can do both just fine."

"Right," I mumbled again.

My wish for no hawks was not to be granted. While descending a hairpin curve in the dirt road, a magnificent redtail swooped not ten feet in front of the windshield.

Brakes jammed.

Gravel spewed.

We peered through the glass to watch the aerial hunter snatch a rabbit that was hunched on the roadside slope. It happened lightning quick. We followed its upward flight, prey tightly clutched in powerful talons. In fascination we watched it disappear into the shadowed forest.

My emotions were swirling in a muddy pool between empathy for the unsuspecting rabbit and awe over the beautiful bird that had gained fresh sustenance. Nature often twisted my emotions and reactions into a triple-knot pretzel. Consequently, I'd found it far wiser to merely *observe* nature, thereby feeling blessed for the many rare sights I'd been gifted with, rather than focusing on specific emotions that had the power to engulf me. This, then, has become an evolutionary response—one born of experiential maturity that served one's emotional preservation during true observation.

Reaching the town of Woodland Park, we stopped off at the bookstore. The owner was babysitting her grandbaby that day and I held him for a bit while walking about and browsing the shelves. After choosing two Colorado wildflower reference guides, I handed the babe over to his grandma and disappeared into the back office to autograph the stock.

After I finished the books, we left and stopped at a fast-food place to pick up carry-out drinks. Leaving Woodland, we began our descent down Ute Pass.

The Pass was a pretty drive, not treacherous like some mountain passes were, but rather a scenic four-lane highway that had just enough curves and hills to make the journey interesting.

Halfway down the Pass, Sally remembered another stop we needed to make.

"I need supplies from the art store," she commented.

"Sure," I responded. Then, "You sure you have time for this project? I can try to get another artist, you know."

"No, it's okay. I'll be all right."

She was a professional artist, and had, in fact, received her college degree in only three years and done a wide variety of highly technical work for national corporations along with book covers and oil portraits of children. Now she was beginning work on over twenty oil paintings for the *Star Babies* book.

She turned and frowned at me. "Why do you keep asking me about these paintings?"

"Because we've got so many projects with the cabin. I don't want you to feel pressured."

"I'll be all right; these take priority over the house projects. Besides, you've got some very specific ideas in your head about how you want these illustrations to look. How could you continually monitor paintings being done by some artist hundreds of miles away? This is your book. It should look exactly how you're envisioning it."

"Okay, I was just checking with you one last time."

"What's after *Star Babies*?" she inquired.

I kept my eyes straight ahead. "*Pinecones and Woodsmoke*," came the immediate reply.

The driver's eyes bored a skeptical glare through me. "Right."

We both knew that specific title was scheduled to be my final book.

"Seriously," she prompted, "what's next?"

"Well, I was thinking that it might be a nice idea to bring my readers into the cabin, make them feel at home. Maybe sitting around the open woodstove in a cozy atmosphere, have them feel like they're right there listening in on one of our eveninglong discussions."

She seemed to mull that over for a time. "I like that. I think they'd love that. What's the title?"

"*Fireside*."

She gave a wry smile. "Don't ask me how I knew that. What about the rest of the trilogy? People are waiting for it. Where do those fit in?"

"There's no need to continue along that vein anymore because that material has already been worked in. *The Visitation* took that necessity away when the archangel covered religious origins, hope for the world, and star relations. That one book laid it all out so I wouldn't have to couch those facts between lines of fiction."

By now we'd reached the art store and, once inside, proceeded to gather the various supplies she needed. Watching the clerk tally the items, I thought how fortunate I was to have so much free work done for a book. This artist never asked for one dime and I believe the thought never entered her mind to do so.

Our next stop was across town at an independent bookstore. The owner was there and made sure that I'd signed all the books that were distributed throughout the store, where she had them stacked on various endcap displays in addition to the regular shelf designation. The three of us visited for the better part of an hour before I took the time to browse for personal reading material. It was my habit to keep at least two books going at one time; one for leisure reading and one for study and research. Lately I'd been drawn to the ancient texts of Nag Hammadi and Qumran.

Pulling out of the bookstore parking lot, we swung into the lot of Houlihan's, where we stopped for lunch. For the first time in my life I tasted quiche. Sally, in one of her subtle attempts to expand my limited worldly horizons, had surreptitiously placed a dollop of hers on the edge of my plate.

Gingerly I'd taken a minuscule amount on the tip of my fork, then more and more portions were tested. I liked it. Previously, I'd been introduced to fresh-baked Italian garlic bread with dipping oil . . . yum. And burritos . . . yuk.

After lunch we headed back through the city for more errands and bookstore stops. By the time we pushed several loaded carts out of Wal-Mart, dusk had descended over the colorful foothills. With bags full of cleaning supplies, bathroom cabinet staples, and bottles of lamp oil filling nearly every available space in the Toyota, we headed back up the pass.

I never failed to breathe a deep sigh of relief at that point, along with a familiar quickening of the heart that always fluttered with the high anticipation of going back home.

In Woodland we stopped to pick up a few grocery items.

In the town of Divide we topped off the gas tank.

From Florissant we turned south on Teller 1. With the evening so crisp and clear, my attention was magnetically drawn to the vast night sky. So many sparkling points of light, some like multicolored beacons or rainbow crystals flashing their alternate rays of red, green, and blue. To me, there was nothing more awe-inspiring than the heavens viewed in their magnificent enormity through the clarity of a high alpine night. It was a priceless blessing I counted.

Reluctantly returning my attention back to the two-lane road, we drove in silence. Occasionally, cars passed us going the other way, many of them homeward bound after a full day of gambling in Cripple Creek.

For several miles we were alone on the dark ribbon of road before the headlights of another northbound car pierced the blackness ahead of us. As this particular vehicle neared the Toyota, its lights outlined the silhouette of a buckboard and two horses in the road in front of it. I noted that the oncoming vehicle wasn't slowing and I was sure the car was going to hit it. If that happened, we'd be alongside right at the point of impact.

Anticipating that Sally would swerve the car out of harm's way, I was about to brace myself, but before I could voice a warning, I saw the oncoming car *pass through the buckboard.*

My scalp crawled.

I was mentally numb.

I snuck a furtive glance over at the driver.

She had her attention on the road ahead.

I thought she hadn't seen what I had seen when, finally, after her own mind settled down, she found her voice. In fact, we both found our voices at the same instant.

"What the *hell* was *that* in the . . . ." she spouted.

"Did you *see* that?" I exclaimed simultaneously as our eyes met.

"What'd *you* see?" she asked.

"You go first," I said. "What'd *you* see?"

Neither of us was willing to admit we'd just seen a phantom out-of-time object on the road, so neither of us responded to the other's question.

As we continued on past Evergreen Station and began to make the snaking ascent toward Cripple Creek, I was deep in thought over how fast the event had happened; even my lightning thought that we'd be involved in the crash if that car hit the . . . the what? And how I'd just reached out in a reflex reaction to brace myself for Sally's swerve onto the shoulder to avoid the expected three-way collision. The speed with which these thoughts and events sped by at the time amazed me.

"An old-time wagon," came the chilling words that shattered the car's icy silence.

I furtively looked over at her. "A brand-new buckboard," I defined.

"Yeah. A buckboard as solid as this car. Those headlights backlighted a *solid* object."

"See anything else?" I asked.

"Legs. The legs of two horses pulling it."

"Me too." I confirmed. "I saw those too, but there were no animal *bodies* attached to them and . . . no driver. No driver was outlined in those car lights."

"Nope. No horse bodies. No driver."

Yet, I thought, that car sped right through it. That car sped right through a solid buckboard standing smack dab in the middle of its lane.

Wanting to verify another detail I'd observed, I asked her if she'd noticed the wood on the buckboard.

"What wood? That thing was dense black. It was like a black cardboard cutout of a silhouette!"

Verification was confirmed.

"That's the one thing that struck me as being really odd about it," I said. "A buckboard on the road out here could be accepted because they use them in Cripple Creek during tourist season, but that one was like a three-dimensional cutout . . . solid black . . . no details anywhere on it. Those headlights only illuminated the solid black outlined form of it."

"And those legs . . . eight horse legs," she reminded.

"And those legs."

"What'd we just see, Mary? What the hell did we just *see* in the road back there?"

"A Time Wrinkle. An imprint. A portal of the Time-Space Continuum. I'm not sure which. One thing I am certain of is the fact that a brand-new buckboard was sitting in that road! When I saw it, it was as real as if a disabled vehicle were sitting there, and I knew you'd have to swerve to avoid an accident."

"Well I *was* getting ready to head for the shoulder. That oncoming vehicle wasn't slowing. I could see it was going to hit the wagon and we needed to get out of the way. But then . . . that car was *through* it before I even had time to react. It was really speeding." Then she smiled. "You know, I've seen some very strange things throughout my life and this is the first time someone else has been able to see the same thing. It's nice."

"Nice," I echoed.

"Yeah, nice."

"Really."

"Really. What, you haven't ever wished that someone else witnessed some of the things you've seen?"

She had me there. "Well . . . yeah."

"Uh-huh. Case closed."

We finished our journey home in silence. I didn't have a definitive explanation for our experience and, although we'd mention it now and again in the future, we pretty much accepted the event and added it to the many other oddities we'd witnessed in life.

Winding down our forested driveway, headlights caught the reflected illumination of various nocturnal critter eyes. The many four-leggeds that called these woods home were constant reminders of nature's living abundance. There were countless wee neighbors sharing the property.

Pulling up to the back of the cabin, the engine silenced and the bright headlight beams were replaced by a wash of silvered moonlight.

Passing through the gate, I was aware of a presence in the forest brush, but then, there were always undergrowth stirrings going on. Yet this time there wasn't the attendant complacency associated with what I'd heard.

Once inside the kitchen door, I touched Sally's arm. "You go down and start the generator, but I'm not letting the dogs into the yard until the floodlights are on."

With flashlight in hand, she opened the basement door. "You think he's out there?"

"Maybe. I just want to make sure it's clear."

"Then wait till I get back upstairs."

The small generator was located beneath the front porch just outside the basement door and, as I waited at the top of the steps, the harsh engine noise shattered the mountain stillness. Behind me the refrigerator began to hum. I switched on the floodlights and, when Sally came back up into the kitchen, she grabbed the .22 and quietly opened the back door.

"You're right," she whispered, "look at 'im."

Sure enough, the massive coyote was boldly sitting not five feet from the fence . . . waiting for the Yorkies.

In a flash my friend was out the door shooting into the ground.

The coyote ran zigzagging off into the night.

Sally came back shaking her head. "If that fellow keeps this up we're going to have to start aiming with the .38."

I hoped we wouldn't have to do that. We kept the .22 on top of the refrigerator so it'd be at the ready to chase off the wild predators with noise. Because coyote packs frequently pierced the night's silence with their yips and howls, I figured any animal killed would simply be replaced by another—eventually. So far the sound of the .22 had done its job.

I let the dogs out and followed them into the lower yard while Sally began unloading the Toyota. If I didn't go down with the dogs, they'd be too intent on greeting us to pay any attention to why they were out there in the first place. Finally they got down to business and then ran in and out the door while I helped empty the vehicle of packages. Never taking long to put everything away, Sally busied herself with starting dinner while I got a fire going in the woodstove. Generator on, dogs out, dinner, and woodstove were parts of our clockwork routine every time we returned home from a day away.

Blue smoke billowed up from the chimney and rose into the moonlight.

The heavily spiced aroma of a well-topped pizza baking filled the kitchen with mouth-watering anticipation.

Dogs, settling down in curled balls of fur, communicated their contentment with finally having everything right with their world again.

This too was felt within my own being. All was right with the world when I was back home. Home. Like E.T., I loved home.

I lit the cedar incense stick and several scented votive candles that I routinely burned each evening. Candlelight had always given a sense of ambient warmth and comfort to the home atmosphere.

Our eating area was a small alcove off the kitchen that had, out of necessity, been converted into my office, where desk, typing table, and file cabinets filled every available space, with no elbowroom to spare; therefore, Sally's maple dining table had to be placed in front of the sliding-glass deck doors. At present it was covered with a wide array of oil paint tubes, palettes, rags, and cans packed with brushes. Beside the table stood her tall easel. This was where she was creating the illustrations for *Star Babies*.

At any one time there were at least five or six Masonite boards propped up around the house to dry, these being paintings in various stages of what I called her works in progress. Consequently, one's lap became the best dining table in the house and we took our steaming pizza into the living room.

I settled in my wing chair beside the picture window that gave a surreal view of the moonlit valley below glittering starshine. After downing a few bites of dinner, I added my voice to that of the crackling fire.

"You didn't mean what you said about replacing the .22 with one of the .38s, did you? I don't want to kill it."

"Neither do I. This was the coyote's territory before we came, still is. Nobody's ever lived in this cabin before we moved in and his pack is used to hunting this valley. All of a sudden there are four little Yorkies out in the yard and he's salivating."

"He's salivating because he needs to eat too. We compromised territory by building that fenced-in area with the poultry wire roof to keep the dogs safe from the hawks and owls so . . . ."

"But the coyotes can jump the gate . . . there's no wire roof over that part."

"Still," I tried, "there's got to be a way we can peaceably coexist, even if I have to go out every time with the dogs. I don't mind shooting off the .22 to chase him away, but we can't actually shoot him." I envisioned the big animal. "He's so beautiful."

"He's also bold," I was reminded. "He was just plain bold the way he sat outside that fence waiting for the little ones."

"He also took off like a shot when you emptied the .22."

She sighed. "Did I tell you what some of the old-timers down at the feed store said when I told them about our coyote?"

I wasn't sure I wanted to hear this. "No. What?"

"Shoot it. They said to shoot it, especially if it comes back after being chased off with gunfire. They said if a coyote is that bold and determined it'll surely 'git them dawgs.'"

I respected the elders' wisdom on the subject and didn't doubt their words, yet I remained silent.

My friend closed the issue. "Mary, let's sit tight and hope our coyote will honor our space as much as you're trying to honor his rights to his."

Mmmm, I would have to talk to our furry wild neighbor and warn him to never attempt a jump over our gate. After all, he did have the whole valley to call his own. I only asked for a little fenced-in yard.

We finished our meal in silence and, when she returned to the living room after taking our plates to the kitchen counter, the subject of sightings was broached. Sally's voice was little more than a whisper.

"Do you remember when we were in the stone cabin and I told you about the crouching wolf I saw there?"

"Wolf."

"Yes."

Yes, something was back in my memory about a wolf she'd mentioned. "That was during the worst of it when I was dealing with violence and threats. That's when I was losing all the weight and was being hit from all sides. My recall of that time is fragmented at best, but I remember something about you telling me of a wolf. The details aren't there though. Sally . . . it's like it all happened in another lifetime."

"But you came through, even your appearance has changed since then."

A smile tipped the corners of my mouth. "Oh yeah, I look different all right; now I've got a lot of gray hair."

She laughed. "That's not what I meant and you know it. You've altered again."

"I noticed," was all I said while remembering the different stages of my facial appearance that were depicted in family albums. "So tell me again about the wolf."

"There's not much to tell. I was coming down the stone steps to your cabin and a black-and-gray wolf was crouching down at the ridge beside the other steps leading down into your woods out front. He was there . . . then he vanished."

"What was your first instinctual impression at the time?" I asked.

"A warning. Danger."

"Those were dangerous times, both physically and emotionally, times full of daily uncertainty. Every stable and solid aspect of my life liquefied beneath my feet. All my realities shattered. Nothing was certain or predictable anymore. Every day new shock waves jarred my life." I shook my head in remembrance. "I can't believe I managed to do the dream book through that time. I think that was amazing."

"It gave you something solid to focus on. You had a deadline for the manuscript and you weren't going to let anyone down. I remember how determined you were about that."

"I don't. All I recall now is that I trudged every day through lists and lists of words; so many words I saw them in my sleep. Well . . . anyway, about your wolf, did I ever mention that I'd seen one too back then?"

She frowned upon hearing my revelation. "No. Where?"

"You know the path beside the cabin that I'd worn through the woods? The one leading down to my prayer circle?"

She nodded.

"Well there were times when I'd be walking up and a large black wolf would be just standing beside the path. This one was all black with yellow eyes. He looked three-dimensional but he wasn't."

"Why didn't you ever tell me about this?"

I shrugged. "What for? He was just one of the many. Appearances of archetypes around the cabin were common."

"And *inside* too," she added with emphasis. "That place was literally crowded some nights. Do you remember me telling you about that little owl that just stood in the corner of the living room some nights when we'd be sitting up late with only your candles burning?"

"I always had candlelight back then, didn't I? They

made a soothing atmosphere for the turmoil I was going through. But yes, I remember that little owl appearing. It was as though it came to give comfort or companionship."

"God, that was a weird time," she recalled, shaking her head. "When I heard that cougar scream come from one of the back rooms it gave me such a cold chill."

I admitted that I'd forgotten about that one.

She shuddered with the memory. "You'd been asleep for a few hours and I'd just pulled the covers over me out on the couch when this wild cat scream came from the back of the house. I couldn't tell whether it'd come from your bedroom or the office. Despite the chills it gave me, I rushed back to check on you; you were sound asleep and the office was dark and empty."

Thinking back on those times, I commented, "You would sit up a lot after I went to bed, wouldn't you?"

"Maybe I shouldn't have. I don't know how many times I felt something touch me, or I'd have the strong sensation that someone was standing behind me. And then I'd be lying on the couch and hear footfalls brush along the carpet. I'd sit up thinking you'd gotten up for something . . . nobody'd be there. I swear, that was the busiest place!"

I smiled. "Sometimes it's like that."

"What blew me away was your complacency about it."

I shrugged. "You get used to that kind of company. If I recall, you began to get less jumpy toward the end. You gained acceptance too."

"Did I have a choice?"

"Of course. Sometimes choices are all we have."

"I didn't have a choice," she insisted. "In my heart, from the depths of my soul, I knew I was exactly where I was supposed to be. As I look back on my life it's clear why certain events happened. Why my two marriage engagements broke off, why I was spared harm from bad accidents. I could go on and on, yet it all comes down to being here—helping you, guarding you and assisting your mission in whatever capacity I can."

"You forgot to mention friend," I said, "being my friend. And you did have a choice; you chose to stay. I don't believe I could've made it through everything without your support."

"You're underestimating yourself. You're strong, a survivor. I believe you'd pull through anything . . . all by yourself."

I had the feeling she was right but had had enough of the subject. Instead of responding, I got up to stoke the fire. The pine we had wasn't quite seasoned enough and it needed aspen to supplement its burn. While I was tending the fire she flipped on the yard floodlights and went out again with the dogs. We were both done at the same time.

∞ ∞ ∞

The fire snapped vigorously while casting bright orange reflections on the knotty pine walls.

I lit a fresh cedar stick and returned to my chair.

Outside, the valley was flooded with quicksilver and my gaze rose to the stars. "I wish you didn't have to do all those paintings," I mused almost under my breath.

"What'd you say?"

I repeated my thought.

"Pretty difficult to create a high-visual children's picture book without having illustrations."

The stars twinkled like sparklers and I had to forcibly pull my gaze away to look back at my friend. "I was hoping for photographs."

Her eyes widened with the shocking realization of what I'd said. "You asked *them* for *photographs* for your book?"

I remained silent. I was feeling foolish for voicing my hopes.

Mentally, she was furiously processing the information I'd just supplied her with.

The pitch in the pine logs snapped and crackled.

Finally my friend spoke, softly. "Mary, you've got to be the most optimistic and trusting person on this earth. What ever made you even think of such a thing?"

"The idea just popped into my mind one day. And why not? What better vehicle than a children's book to have interplanetary collaboration on? It's time. It would've been a gentle way for them to present actual photos of their planets and people."

"Gentle? Gentle! You haven't thought this out! Jeez, Mary, you have not thought this out!" She was so perturbed over my idea that she began to pace before the woodstove. "Photos. Actual *photos* given to you?"

"Yes."

"Okay," she began to hypothesize, "say they did this. How would the book get past the printer, whose eyeballs would bug at the photos? You think for one minute anyone seeing those would keep quiet?"

Silence.

"Huh?"

"I didn't think about that."

"Uh-huh. So this printer maybe has a friend in the government or maybe he sees dollar signs and calls a tabloid. There's no way that book would reach publication without the government stopping it. Then,

then you've got military types all over you wanting to know how the photos were made, if they're real and, if so, where'd they come from? Or else the Men In Black come calling. You think for one minute your people 'up there' would want you in that position? You may have thought it was a gentle way for that kind of project cooperation, but I'm sure *they* don't see it that way." She sighed heavily. "God, you're so trusting. How could you even contemplate doing something that would prove to be the most dramatic revelation of the century?"

"I didn't see it like that," I quietly confessed. "I saw it as a beautiful way for the various star civilizations to present reality."

Her voice softened. "Oh, Mary, you do need looking after. You've got to lower the frequency of your thought process more often; it's so spiritually 'up there' that you don't even think to consider the baser ramifications and backlash coming from the 'down here' society. I'm sorry that's the way it is down here, but don't you see? If you and they did something like this you'd never have another moment of privacy or peace for the rest of your life."

"I need to remain low-key, in the background . . . behind the word," I gently expressed.

"I know," she whispered.

Musing, I voiced my thought. "It was such a good idea. I was excited about the possibility and had such faith that it could be done. I mean . . . why not? I saw no reason why it couldn't be accomplished. Well . . . now I do. I should've taken it further. I guess it wasn't such a beautiful idea after all."

She'd returned to her place on the couch. "It *was* a beautiful idea. What turned it sour was the certainty of the government's rash response to it. You would've finally presented the public with proof of its cover-ups."

I didn't respond.

We sat in silence then, each attending to her private thoughts on the issue.

I had jumbled feelings. It was still a beautiful idea, yet my friend was absolutely right about the trouble I'd bring on if the photos were used. That kind of overreactive response is precisely what made my work so difficult here. Clearly it held me back. It restricted my words and projects; consequently, there was an aspect of frustration caused by certain elements of earthly societal segments. This specific instance led me to recall another that had recently invaded my life when I'd received a book in the mail written by a religious radical. In it, six pages were devoted to denigrating my life and publications. It clearly stated that I was doing the work of the devil and, if I wasn't stopped, I'd prove to be a strong force for Satan in the world. What pained me most about this author's words was when he falsely claimed that, when my grandma appeared to me at the end of my bed so many years ago . . . she was actually Satan in disguise. I now shook my head at the memory of such misguided statements.

"What's wrong?" came the question from across the room.

"Oh, I was thinking about that book I'd received in the mail, the one claiming I was working for Satan."

"I'm sorry about that one. What made you start thinking on that?"

"People's various reactions to my work brought me to that." I shook my head once again. "With all I've said about the beauty of God's beingness evidenced in nature, it blows my mind how anyone can claim that Satan is behind my words. God and goodness has been the underlying theme of all my messages. It seems to me that I must be doing something wrong for even one person to conclude that I'm an agent of a dark one."

Her voice was almost commanding. "Don't go there. Don't you dare go there. You've helped thousands of people through your work. You've changed the lives of countless readers worldwide. You've given others encouragement by the example of your own perseverance. You've shown . . . ."

"Wait a minute," I interrupted. "My *words* have done all that . . . my *message*. Don't confuse the message with the messenger."

"Hello?" she shot back. "Last time I looked, words didn't put themselves on paper. Your words, your message, come from *your* mind, *your* heart and spirit. *Your* thoughts and life experiences changed people's lives."

"Now you're muddying up my most basic tenet of separation of message from messenger. You of all people know how strongly I feel about that."

"Yes, I do, yet the fact remains that *you* presented the words. Do you dispute that?"

"You're getting way too simplistic," I said, avoiding the question.

"Am I? I *am*? I thought simplicity is what your message is all about?"

"Now you're turning my own words back on me."

Her brow rose. "Turning? Turning or asking you to look at your own words? Mary, you can't get away from the fact that it's human nature to appreciate the person whose words changed one's life. I'm not talking about making a goddess of the messenger, I'm talking about plain and simple gratitude."

I smiled. "Well, that's different then, isn't it. Now we're on the same page. The feeling of appreciation is a natural reciprocal response. I too appreciate certain people in my life: my readers, the blessings I count on a daily basis."

Sally smiled back. "Okay then, we've established that it's permissible to appreciate one who changes your life for the better . . . ." She hesitated then. "What got us on this subject to begin with?"

I chuckled. "That book did. People's opinions. Personal perspectives."

"You might call it by those terms," she said, "but I'd call that libel or slander."

"Clearly that author really believes his twisted theory," I said. "And if that's the case, he's drawing the wrong conclusions—his own personal assumptions—and then presenting them to the public as though they were indisputable facts. Everyone has a right to express an opinion on anything they choose. The problem arises when folks can't or don't discern the difference between fact and opinion. Although this person is of the opinion I'm working for Satan, he presented it as solid fact."

"And," she added, "people who never heard of you will read his words and think you should be stopped. That alone suggests a spiritual call to action against you."

I mumbled. "It wouldn't be the first time."

She sighed in exasperation. "I mean in *this* life. Will you get serious about this? The way I see it, no matter how you behave, no matter how you present your message, someone somewhere is going to color it with their own spin. You can't please everyone and . . . ."

"I'm not trying to please anyone, I only . . . ."

"Well, what I meant was you can't expect everyone to internalize—interpret—your words in the same way."

"There's no interpreting required. Simplicity, remember? No workbooks needed to figure out what I've said. God speaks in plain language, so does the messenger, otherwise . . . why bother? There'd be no point. And that fact brings me to a good example of this whole interpretation issue.

"The gospels of the apostles each have variations of biblical history in the time of Jesus. Different biblical texts also vary greatly, depending on which translated version one picks up to read. And now, now enters the Nag Hammadi and Qumran scrolls unearthed from hidden cave pottery and, what do you know, *these* contain some completely *different* versions of that ancient time. But!" I exclaimed, raising a cautionary finger, "all the modern day scholars are currently involved in impassioned infighting over whose translation of these is right. They can't even agree if the scrolls are written about Jesus or the spiritual leader of the Essene sect. The scholars are individually publishing criticisms of each other's theories! So . . . what *does* work? I published personal life journals written by my own hand and what do we see? We see me already being misquoted in regard to the historical facts of my life. That one personal example shows how easy it is for facts to be altered. Makes you wonder how many facts were changed, deleted, or expanded upon when the apostles sat down to record their time with a famous person, doesn't it?"

"So write a *correct* gospel," came her reply.

"I'm not here to write new gospels or rewrite old ones; I just point to the horizon in as many different ways as I can. People need to think on things more. Deeper. Contemplate. I'm here to make them think."

Silence hung between us while my friend composed a response.

Pinecone jumped on my chair and curled up in my lap. My fingertips smoothed the silkiness of her silver head, which wasn't much larger than a golf ball.

Then, my friend managed to capture the singular thread of my thought that exemplified the futility of writing a corrected version of the gospel.

"No new gospel could be proven until the scrolls of Jesus' mother are discovered," she stated.

I'm not sure the firelight illuminated my confirming expression enough for her to see it. "Yes, her diary; yet even then, when those are found, the scholars will keep them secreted away for years, just like the Dead Sea Scrolls were. They'll probably spend more years translating them into their own individualized versions too."

"Oh for God's sake," she spewed with growing disgust. "I suppose they'll even argue over who wrote those too."

A smile tipped the corners of my mouth. "I don't think so. Hers are different."

My friend cocked her head in question.

"Hers," I said, "are written in the ancient language of Jesus' own tongue. Hers are in Aramaic."

We let that fact rest between us for a few moments, neither commenting further.

The conversation sparked to life again when my friend returned to something I'd recently said. "I want to go back to what you said about being here to make people think . . . ."

"I worded that badly," I immediately corrected. "I'm not here to *make* anyone do anything. I'm here to *encourage*, act as a catalyst toward deeper thought," I clarified.

"I knew that. You don't have to be so precise with me."

"I need to be precise with myself, no matter who I'm talking with. Words are too powerful. One imprecise term and you end up with all sorts of misinterpretations."

She gave a slightly exasperated sigh. "I never saw anyone who could take one idea down so many roads. Can I get back to my original thought now?"

"Go for it," I playfully urged.

The firelight caught the sparkle of her eyes as she shook her head. "My issue is with you *encouraging* people to think deeper. One of your books was written for that specific purpose and, from what I've seen, people perceive it as just a nice la-de-da travelogue of Colorado–a pretty gift book."

"Mmmm, yes. The words got lost somehow. So did the intent of it."

"Mary, *Whispered Wisdom* is just that . . . wisdom to contemplate. Your original intent to add visual beauty to the philosophical ideas has backfired. People's initial impression of the book is 'a pretty,' an unnecessary or frivolous volume of your series, yet it's so full of important concepts, even a few solutions to certain mysteries couched in colorful prose. It's a serious work."

"They're all serious works. *Pinecones and Woodsmoke* will be different, though," I assured.

That perked her interest. "Oh? Now what creative ideas are rolling around in that busy head of yours?"

"Not more photographs, that's for sure. I've already accumulated over four hundred pages of thoughts typed on that book; can't very well add a photo to go with each one."

"So?" she prompted.

"So?" I echoed.

"So, c'mon, what's your idea for it?"

I didn't answer her right away. I hesitated.

She patiently waited.

Finally I detailed my idea.

Though highly unusual, she liked the plan.

"That would make a precious gift of yourself to your readers. They'll love it."

Something in her voice led me to think she was holding back. "Why do I feel you're reserving a 'but' in there somewhere?"

"I just don't think you realize how much work it's going to involve for you."

"You're probably right. I'm still going to try it though, because this idea has a stranglehold on me and I've the feeling it won't ease up until I've at least given it an honest shot."

"It's going to be beautiful," she commented.

"We'll see."

Sally then reached to open the top drawer of the couchside table. She pulled out a brush and began grooming the little Yorkie curled in her lap. Baby was soon dosing beneath the gentle strokes.

After a time, I said, "What's truth?"

"Excuse me?" she responded with surprise.

"What . . . is . . . truth?" I repeated.

"What kind of question is that?"

"A valid question."

"I mean, coming from you, that's an odd question."

"No, it's not. I want to know what truth is, spiritual truth."

"This sounds like a trick question. I'm not sure what you mean."

Pinecone began twitching in her sleep. I soothed her as Punkin and Rosie nestled down on either side of me.

"Maybe it's a trick subject, convoluted," I suggested. "We were both raised with very rigid Catholic dogma, truths that were as solid as rock. Then, at a young age, we both began to question those truths because too many elements didn't fit with our inner knowing. Add to that the changes in dogma the Church began making and the former truths are shattered; therefore, the truths couldn't have been truths to begin with.

"The spiritual truths of all the various established religions differ from one another in range from great to negligible, yet the members of each sect emphatically believe their set of truths are the Truth. How can that be if they vary so much?

"The Bible," I further explained, "was written by so many diverse people having an equally expansive range of opinions and perspectives that alterations through embellishments and deletions stand out in the gospels alone. Can we declare with absolute certainty that the dream scenario of Revelations wasn't merely a simple disjointed recall of a dream? Or was it a fabricated story? Or perhaps it was a bona fide message given through symbology?

"Enter now the Dead Sea Scrolls, which have been an unremitting bone of contention among the very so-called scholars who've been entrusted with the task of deciphering them for years. Not even two of them can agree on one singular translation, nor can they make a definitive pronouncement as to who wrote them or conclude what historical character the scrolls are referring to. What is the truth of the scrolls if the scholars have conflicting interpretations?"

"You've given this a lot of thought, haven't you?"

"Well it's clear that a truth would be one that's incontrovertibly solid, so much so that everyone believes in its indisputable quality. It's *recognizable* as an unequivocal fact. How many such incontestable facts can you enumerate? Even if I said something as basic as 'God is good,' would that be an unshakable fact? No, it wouldn't be, because atheists don't even believe in an entity defined or recognized as God. So then, reducing this issue down to its most base component leaves us with a resulting residue of what?"

"Personal perspective. Opinion," she immediately responded.

"Exactly. And a multitude of variant perspectives, opinions, translations, and outright denials associated with one specific idea cannot determine or indisputably define a truth. Oh sure, you and I believe God is good; we also believe God created all life; but what of the evolutionists?"

"Well then," she posed, "various spiritual beliefs make up one's *personal* spiritual truths . . . what they *call* their truths."

"That's just it, isn't it? *Their* truths. How can such an animal exist? Isn't that a contradiction? A misnomer if *everyone* doesn't recognize it as being truth? I'm not referring to variances in terminology either. I understand that the table over there could be called a credenza, a commode, a stand, or whatever, but it's still recognizable to everyone as some type of table. I'm talking about the *facts* of the spiritual realm and not a single one can be found to be free from possible dispute by *someone*. My question is this: Why? Is it that human nature compels one to put her or his own spin on the facts, thereby creating a plethora of individualized belief systems? We both saw something on the road coming home tonight. We know what we saw and experienced; that is our truth of it. It was truth as we saw it, yet how many people would believe that 'truth' if we shared the event with them? Same with the UFOs we've both seen up close, yet those are examples of truths proven out through personal experiential life events and, unless all others living on this planet have similar encounters, *our* truth will not be accepted as an indisputable truth to all. See? So where are the indisputable spiritual truths?" I glanced out into the night. "Nobody would dispute that those stars are celestial bodies. That's truth. Why are the most important truths of all relegated to speculation, opinion, and individualized perspective or experiential events? Why aren't they as bright as those glittering stars?"

"I don't think I have an answer. In lieu of one I'd have to say faith would be the closest I could come. What you're asking isn't what is truth, but rather where is the *proof* of spiritual truth? Without solid, touchable truths, people believe on faith alone. Is it really so important that there's no one world spiritual belief based on completely indisputable, touchable spiritual truths?"

I didn't answer.

She continued her line of thought. "Don't most religious/spiritual sects teach goodness and right living? Isn't that the bottom line? Aren't the Ten Commandments pretty much a set of ground rules to guide people's general behavior? Are you looking for a spiritual Utopia here on earth?"

"I'm looking for evidence of spiritual truth in the world and all I've been able to find is opinions and contradictory translations."

"You're looking for a unicorn, a Pegasus."

"What I'm looking for is *why* it's a unicorn or Pegasus. *Why*?"

No answer came back to me, probably because there was none.

I gently lifted Pinecone off my lap and set her down on the chair. Stoking the fire and adding a mix of pine and aspen, my mind continued to meander along the stream of our conversation. By our own personal experiences I saw how truth was manifested through the evidence of experiential events in one's life. What Sally and I saw and experienced as solid reality, others would scoff at, at least until they too saw and experienced the identical events. Did that mean truth could only be undisputed by everyone if it were seeable? Touchable? No, because I then considered the ultimate spiritual evidence and the concept came up short. If the beingness of God materialized out of the sky for all to see, some would believe it was mass hysteria or Satan being busy deceiving the world.

Sally took advantage of our break by refreshing our drinks and letting the dogs out. By the time we were settled again we both realized the former issue was played out.

"You know, Mary," she began in a voice heavy with compassion. "It sounds like what you're wanting to see is a humanity unified in its spiritual belief and personal relationship with God."

That statement settled it for me. "You just described heaven."

"I know," she whispered, "that's where your proof of spiritual truth lives."

The three little dogs repositioned themselves around me as they were before. Baby snuggled back into Sally's lap. Cheyenne took the guard position beside my chair.

The room was toasty warm and the pine walls glowed with the luster of orange ember light.

The scent of cedar permeated the air.

I exhaled a heavy sigh of contentment. "This is so nice," I said. "So incredibly peaceful."

"You traveled a long way in a relatively short time," came the response.

"I've never known such peace." I indulged my beingness in the touchable tranquillity for a few golden moments before I spoke again. "I've made a shocking observation about my life now. Having been married for twenty-nine years conditioned me to always think of my mate, consider another's opinion for decision-making, etc. This is the first time in my life that I feel like an individual. Do you know what I mean?"

She nodded.

"I'm now a 'me' instead of a 'we.' It took a while for me to realize what that meant."

"Did that realization seem scary or make you nervous?" she asked.

"No, it felt wonderfully liberating. That probably sounds like I'm inferring that marriage was restrictive, but I'm not saying that at all. There's a brand-new feeling of freedom and independence when one's decisions or plans are suddenly solely their own to make. No more asking or compromising with a partner—those aren't there anymore. It finally dawned on me that I can do anything or go anywhere I want. My life is no longer contingent on another. There's nobody saying 'no' anymore. Please don't misinterpret what I'm saying here. I'd always believed I'd have the same mate forever, but since that wasn't to be, I'm simply noticing how my life has altered."

"You don't have to defend your words to me," she said, "facts are facts and, the fact is, you now find yourself totally independent for the first time in your life. I imagine it would take some getting used to."

"It's an amazement to me actually. The feeling is so foreign. I'd always identified myself through the joint beingness of a 'we' and suddenly I'm an 'I'!"

That made her grin.

"You think that's funny?" I asked through a like grin.

"No, not funny . . . amusing's more like it. How's it feel to be an individual?"

"Strange. Just the other day I realized that I could pick up stakes and move to another state if I wanted or sell this house and spend the rest of my days traveling the country in an RV."

"You're your own person, Mary. You can do whatever you're inspired to do."

"That's just so extraordinary to me." Then, "Why are you shaking your head?"

"You. You've just discovered you're a person instead of a pair. Some people would think that's hilarious."

"Or pitiful," I added. "Some would think that's sad."

"Now, now," she cautioned, "we've just left the issue of other people's perspectives and opinions, we don't need to go there again. What's important is how *you* feel about your life now. Right?"

I smiled. "Peaceful. I came out okay."

∞ ∞ ∞

For a while we basked in the calm ambiance of the room. There was nothing to disturb the contentedness I felt surrounding me. I glanced out the window. The disk of the moon was in full view now. The hillocks of the valley below were clearly defined with illumination.

"Do you think I'm a hermit?" I wondered aloud.

"Oh God, where'd that come from? No, I don't think you're a hermit. You go out whenever you want, don't you?"

"Of course, but that's not very often. I'd rather be right here. Why leave where I want to be most? Why go someplace else if this is where I feel most at peace?"

"You're asking me?"

"I wasn't really asking, more like explaining. I brought up the hermit thing because it seems that everyone is trying to tell me what I should be doing, as if I'm a prisoner here or not free to go out. Everyone has a different opinion regarding what I should be doing; one person keeps trying to get me to travel and see the world. Well, I don't especially like traveling. Another friend keeps harping about being more outgoing—social. Well I'm not comfortable in social situations and I hate having to drive somewhere. Know what?"

"What?"

"Nobody ever asked me what I want to do. Isn't that odd? They all think I should be doing what they like to do. What I want to do most is stay right here in this quiet valley filled with wildlife, where I feel so totally at peace and *that,* I know, would drive all of them stir crazy. Why is it that I'm perceived as a hermit or being antisocial if I don't like doing what they like to do? Reverse it. Maybe they seem odd for not wanting to stay where it's peaceful."

"You're not a hermit, Mary, and you're not odd. You prefer a . . . cloistered kind of life because it's naturally more aligned with who you are within—your raw beingness. You're not a worldly person, you're a solitary person and there's absolutely nothing wrong with that. People who can't see that aren't respecting your unique individuality. They think you should be like them, do what they do, enjoy the same things they do. Your differentness bothers them."

"Why?"

"There are most likely a lot of personal answers to that. You'd have to ask them."

"It's not that important for me to know. We're different; maybe someday they'll realize that fact and finally accept it. Right now they don't see me as being the same as I've always been, a homebody. When I was married, people were used to seeing me in social situations as a pair where my highly talkative mate carried the conversation. I was usually just along for the ride. He was the extrovert, a people person, and seemed to crave having others around him, while all I needed was him. He was my best friend. Now that I'm alone, people are seeing me for the first time and, with the extrovert half of the former pair gone, they think I've changed. But I haven't, I'm still the same quiet and solitary person I've always been." I caught Sally's eye at this point. "I feel some people think you're the one who's encouraging my stay-at-home attitude."

"Some of them haven't been very discreet about their opinion. Seems I'd been judged and sentenced before they'd even met me."

"That's so unfair. I'm so sorry about that. People believe what they want to believe no matter what the facts are."

"Well," she soothed, "they just never really knew you as an individual, Mary. They always saw you with an extrovert so, therefore, you must be one too. It's okay."

"No it's not. It's got to hurt your feelings."

She shrugged it off. "I'm not here for them. Besides, it's your feelings that count."

"I don't agree."

"That's your right."

"Well their prejudiced attitude is bothering me a lot. It's alienating me from them."

"Don't let it do that, Mary. Their attitudes come from ignorance and never having understood or known the real you."

"Well . . . it's so unfair and cruel to treat . . ."

"Let it go."

I let the dialogue on this issue conclude; yet inside, I was nearly seething about the situation. Outright unkindness, rudeness, and cattiness due to gossip and false judgments were difficult for me to ignore. I didn't need these kinds of people in my life.

My perceptive friend most likely saw the steam shooting out my ears as I silently stewed. She changed the subject. "There was an article in the paper about an upcoming celestial event. What do you think about it?"

"You're interrupting my thoughts," I grumbled.

"*Distracting* is what I'm doing," she corrected. "You don't need those anyway. So, what do you think about this event?"

I looked out into the velvet night. "It's going to be interesting."

She waited to hear more.

More wasn't expressed.

"It'll be interesting," I repeated.

"That's it? That's all you have to say about it?"

"What more is there to say? You asked what my opinion was and I gave it." I grinned then. "What you want me to comment on is what I think other people's opinions are about it. Clearly a great many are going to see it as a bad omen or some type of hoodoo sign. It's neither of those things. It's nothing but a celestial event, one of hundreds that are ongoing all the time; difference is, this one we'll be able to see because of its proximity to earth. People have no conception of the total size of the universe, therefore, they lose sight of the fact that celestial events are continually manifesting everywhere in that vastness of the universe, completely unobserved, and no one is the wiser. So, because we get to observe this particular event, people tend to attach some sort of esoteric significance to it and, suddenly . . . the sky is falling."

"End of the world kind of thing," she clarified.

"Sure. Doesn't that come into play every time something happens that could even remotely be viewed as some type of portent? The human race never outgrew its primitive craving for superstitions. Seeing an unusual celestial alignment makes them think the sky's falling. I don't see any evidence of the intelligence it takes to realize that certain physiological changes have been in process for decades. The apocalypse has been in process for a long while. Bit by bit, one event following another, pigment by added pigment, the entire painting is being created. They're not seeing that. They're waiting for it all to culminate at once in some dramatic manner so they can point to it and, without question or hesitation, declare: End Times!"

"So, in the meantime," Sally said, "every out-of-the-ordinary event, such as this one, is perceived as an End Times harbinger."

"Yes. When the big one finally hits California they'll claim the same thing, just watch. Yet, in reality, that will simply be one more event that's adding to create the whole picture, which has been developing for years now. The End Times is nothing more than a cleansing process to *end* certain diseased aspects of earth. It's a realignment, so to speak, an adjustment or correction period. Due to the earth's natural physiology, there's always going to be adjustments made to alleviate pressure and stress buildup, which are evidenced through the earthquakes and volcanoes. These are natural events that serve to correct the earth's mantle surface tension. These are necessary events our planet must experience for it to maintain general stability.

"Planetary alignments are one minuscule aspect of our vast universe. They're a natural celestial element. To entertain the idea that they're a sure sign of the End sounds absolutely ludicrous to me. It brings to mind neanderthal or medieval thinking. Overall, I anticipate a wide range of outlandish and bizarre beliefs bringing about rash, reactive behavior with this event."

Sally interjected a comment. "I've heard that there are some who believe a mother ship will appear with this alignment."

"Are you kidding me?" I exclaimed. "Seems we've heard that one before."

She shook her head. "No, I'm not kidding you. Some really believe that again."

"Where on earth do they get that idea? Why, that's got to be right up there among the dumbest things I've ever heard. We heard that story when Hale-Bopp came along. That's not even a logical theory. Every high-powered telescope in observatories all across the country will be trained on the night sky, even highly sophisticated satellites that can get fine resolution will be watching it."

"I don't know where ideas like that come from," she added. "But I saw a book about it being an End Time harbinger . . . an omen."

"Feed the frenzy," I mumbled to myself.

"What? What'd you say?"

"Feed the frenzy. Feed people's uncertainty with fear and give them something else to fret and beat their breasts over. Even a meteor, if large enough, will wipe out everything anyway. Everyone will be gone and so be it. Why worry? Why worry about something as final as that would be? These kinds of fears only prevent people from living a good and full daily existence. These fears of the future only serve to overshadow their beautiful daily blessings." I shook my head. "In the final analysis, these corny ideas, all of them, are going to lead people to opting out on life. If they see nothing in the world's future but darkness and devastation, they're going to sink into a black depression and see no purpose to life.

Their entire outlook will be skewed so badly that they won't have the rationale to peer through that darkness to see the wrongness of their thinking.

"A planetary alignment, no matter how rare, is nothing in relation to this upcoming millennium date. Like the alignment, it will simply be another natural event–just one more counted year added to all the ones preceding it. But watch the craziness explode. That date holds no uniqueness to me. It's no spooky omen. No dark portent. And, God willing, I plan to grow old . . . very old. Yet people fear the millennium. And it will be their fears that will destroy them. Superstition feeds many. It makes some rich. It controls people's lives. It can even kill them. The closer to the millennium we get, you're going to see a multitude of the Ego People manipulating others through their powerful and clever use of superstition. The Ego People maintain a firm hold over others through fear."

I continued talking while I got up and lit another incense stick. "The future and the fear of it has become an all-consuming subject. It's as though the very idea of God and having confidence in God's love for us has fallen by the wayside. You know what I mean?"

My friend nodded. "Wanting to know the future has become more important than living the moment."

"Yes. Yes, that's exactly my point. There's no more joy or appreciation of the moment anymore. Worries and fears of the future have preoccupied people's minds."

"What about *Phoenix Rising?*"

"What about it?"

"That book frightened a few people."

I thought on that. "*Phoenix Rising* was a wake-up call. Many of the specific predictions were associated with personal awareness and taking individual responsibility, not only for the actions of self, but also for those of others—but always in relation to being aware of what's transpiring around one. The book served to put people on their toes and be watchful—more observant of their world. Don't forget, that book also ended on a note of hope. It concluded with a cleansed and renewed planet, where people appreciated and respected their relationships with it and all of life. It represented a cleansing-process scenario, not a definitive End Time one."

"It still scared people."

"I don't doubt it did. Sometimes a little jarring out of complacency or apathy is needed as a call to greater awareness and responsibility. I saw the book as giving folks choices. Being forewarned and informed provides opportunities to make knowledgeable decisions. For example, if one knows there's going to be a marked increase in air travel accidents, one can choose to take a chance or opt for an alternative form of travel. Likewise, being apprised of questionable geographic regions highlights the more stable areas to reside in."

"And here you sit," she grinned, "on the rim of an ancient caldera."

"And here I sit," I repeated with a resigned smile. "I also never told people to run to the more secure regions. I advise them to be wherever they're prompted to be. This place, because of the circumstances that led me here, was provided for me at this time in my life. It's given me great solace and deep peace. Tomorrow or next week or two years from now I may be led somewhere else, yet that's in the future and I live one day at a time . . . in the now. What will be, will be. The variant elements of each day get handled as they come."

The corner of my mouth tipped up. "Each new day is like opening a gift-wrapped present, you thank the almighty Giver for it then . . . see what you've received."

"That's a beautiful way to look at life."

"It took a while to get there," I admitted, "and now I see that it's the most comforting, rewarding, and grounded perspective one could have."

"We're back to the idea of living the moment," she pointed out.

"So we are. Each moment can be an overflowing cup or it can be completely empty. Which one it ultimately ends up being is solely determined by one's choice of personal perspective . . . attitude."

"Still," she added, "the future can't be absolutely ignored. It's important, too."

"I wouldn't argue with that because it has its place in the overall scheme of life. Without an eye on the future there'd be no plans made, no life direction, no goals or objectives to reach for and strive toward. Yet there's a right and wrong perspective that comes into that equation, too. The *future* simmers on the *back* burner while the *present* is today's fine meal that is tended to on the *front* burner."

"Where do you come up with those visual analogies of yours?"

I shrugged. "That one just slipped out on its own. Kind of surprised me too, but it made the simple point, didn't it. Actually," I half hinted, pointing to my head, "I have this very wise elder up here who frequently shares her thoughts."

"Well, clear and simple is *your* style."

"Hers too. We're one and the same."

Letting my meaning slide past her, she commented, "As I said, clear and simple is your style. Isn't that the basis of all your messages?"

"It isn't always easy, but I try," I responded, "I try to keep to the bottom line."

∞ ∞ ∞

I watched Rosie prance over to the toy box in the corner of the room. She rummaged around in it until she proudly extracted her favorite blue Koosh ball and anxiously set it on the edge of the love seat. Rosie, brimming with barely contained anticipation, sat at Sally's feet. When the pup got no immediate response, she nosed Sally's hand, then inched the ball a millimeter closer before sitting at heightened attention again.

With lightning speed, the ball was grabbed up and thrown before Rosie could snap it up. She returned in a flash with it and, once more, set it on the edge of the couch, nosing it and the hand when attention wasn't promptly given to it.

While Sally played throw and fetch and Punkin unsuccessfully tried to reach the ball before Rosie, our conversation continued.

My friend introduced a new subject. "The owner of the bookstore wants a photograph for your appearance."

I was scheduled to autograph books for an independent bookstore. I'd agreed to it only because it wasn't too far to travel . . . in Denver at the Tattered Cover.

"Photograph?"

With the strength behind her old fast ball, the toy was pitched into the kitchen.

Rosie was a blur across the carpet after it.

Punkin halfheartedly made an attempt.

"It's the usual PR," she said. "They always want an advertising photo and we need to get them one."

"I don't have any."

Her brows knitted together. "What are all those eight-by-tens in the file drawer then?"

She referred to the photographs that were taken to accommodate the bookstore requests for the cross-country signing trip we'd done a couple of years earlier. The photographing session took place during the worst time in my life and she'd nearly had to stand on her head to elicit some semblance of a smile out of me then. As it was, I could find fewer than six photographs that I thought were passable out of the many rolls of film we shot. A few ended up in *Bittersweet.*

"I don't want to use any of those," I said. "They represent a terrible time."

"She needs one now. Why don't you pick out one from what we have, just for this one time, then we can take a new set."

The ball was tossed in my lap.

Rosie skidded across my legs.

I snapped up the ball and handed it off to Punkin Pie, who was now diligently trying for it. Punkin guarded her new treasure with warning growls at Rosie. It wouldn't be long before Rosebud had control of the prize again . . . it never was, but Punkin often needed a little intervention to compensate for Rosie's incredible speed.

I agreed to choose a photo for the signing. As for taking a new set, I gave that some thought while Sally resumed the fetch game. Rosie had already regained possession.

I didn't relish the idea of doing another photo session because I didn't like having my picture taken. Yet I needed to work within the framework of the business end of my occupation and, providing public relations and current advertising material was an unavoidable element of it. I didn't want to use ten-year-old photographs, nor was the *Bittersweet* set acceptable to me anymore.

"Gosh, I hate the thought of doing new ones," I moaned.

"Since you don't want to use what we have, we've no choice," she concluded while pitching the ball into my chair.

This time I picked up Punkin and held the ball for her. She snuggled down in my lap—the 'safe' zone—and protected it from Rosie.

I admitted that the set we had not only signified a difficult period in my life, but it also had an ethnic aspect and, in addition, seemed as though it were an entire lifetime away.

"I was passing through a major transition stage back then," I said. "So much has changed. I've grown so far past any kind of ethnic aspect associated with my work and message. All that seems like it took place in another life."

My friend had witnessed the entire process of my transition period and wholeheartedly agreed. "I'm not sure 'transition' adequately describes what you passed through. I see it more accurately defined as an 'evolutionary' process. Look around the cabin. You've given a good amount of your native things away. Without ever realizing it, you've shed most of the extraneous earth-related elements of your life. What remains is the soul of you. Your life, your work, you, have shed everything that's not spiritually relevant in order to simplify your existence." She smiled. "You've left the cocoon behind. When was the last time you wore one of your serapes?"

"I don't remember," I admitted with surprise. "I suppose it was when we took the winter PR set of photographs. It's been a while, I guess." As I gave thought to my regular attire, I realized that, for over two years now, I'd either worn flannel shirts with Levi's and tennis shoes or peasant blouses with long country skirts. Most of my native wear had either been given away or folded up in the cedar chest for a long time.

To further underscore the depth of this transformation of mine, Sally asked me why I wasn't wearing any turquoise jewelry anymore.

The question stunned me. "I never noticed."

"You put all your turquoise and native-type jewelry in a separate jewelry box. Now you only wear the antique style that's in the small case."

"You're right. I guess it's all related. I've been wearing what feels most comfortable . . . what's me."

"Your new photographs will reflect your new simplified essence, you know."

"You think so?"

"It's who you are. Without the ethnic clothing that colored your image and, in some ways, narrowed your message, you'll be letting the pure spirit shine forth unencumbered."

I liked the sound of that. I liked it a lot. "Remember the man who came to a book signing and expressed his disappointment to see my hair tied back?"

She nodded. "He was in expectation over your appearance. He expected to see your hair loose . . . like an Indian woman's."

"Mmmm. I think these new photos will be a good thing after all. People need to see the soul of me . . . not a serape or turquoise jewelry."

"The soul of you was always seen in your eyes," she reminded.

"Maybe so, yet now they won't be in expectation in regard to my physical appearance or how I'm dressed. There were a couple of times when I wanted to wear Levi's and a flannel shirt to book signings because I felt most comfortable dressed like that. It was more me, if you know what I mean."

"Sure I do. So, why didn't you, if that's what you wanted to do?"

"There were those around me who didn't think it was appropriate attire for an autographing appearance."

"You need to be you . . . wherever you are."

"Those were my sentiments too, still are. I think the ethnic accents I once gave to clothing and accessories aligned with where I was at during that developmental phase of my personality. It was sort of a required experience needed to recapture and integrate a specific facet of my beingness. Now I've accomplished that and grown, or moved on, or evolved. The precise term for it isn't important to me. I just know that I'm somewhere different now. It's so far removed from where I used to be that the times with my old teacher are like trying to recall a fuzzy childhood dream or piece together fragments from a past life. She was one element of my past and is far from defining the totality of who I am."

"Does it bother you when people ask about her now?"

"Only because my time with her has become so distant and I've grown so much since then, only when folks attempt to define my beingness through her. I am an individual unto myself. She was one unique facet comprising a small portion of my entire experiential history. Her words represented a fraction of the total message I'm here to give. One's identity is not defined by a teacher or singular experience. One's identity is unique and composite, a composite of angled facets making up the beautiful crystal that is one's total personality . . . one's individuality." Expressing these thoughts aloud brought me to a related issue.

"This subject matter, of integrating one's ethnicity into the totality of their beingness to create a whole personality, reminds me of one of my reader's comments about not using Carole Bourdo's Indian artwork for my book covers anymore. This is all tied in to my evolution into totality. I want the spiritual message to be universal and not give the impression that it's connected to any kind of ethnic slant. Therefore, I need book covers that convey a generalized depiction of the book's content rather than one giving the reader the idea that it's related to an Indian culture or philosophy.

"Besides," I added, "Carole mentioned that she'd like to be semiretired from her artwork. She's also in New Zealand for nearly eight months of the year."

"You've evolved out of the ethnic aspect of your life but the name remains."

"Yes. The name. Now and then I've given that some consideration, too."

"You mean *change* it?"

I didn't respond.

"Mary, if you changed your name and still wrote books, who would know they came from you?"

"Who needs to know?"

"You can't be serious."

"It's the words that are important, not the name of the messenger. Besides, a different name would help maintain the anonymity I'm striving for."

"Only if you moved to an entirely different geographic region, maybe. Everywhere you go around here you're known by your appearance. It's your face, your hair, people recognize. A name change can't conceal your identity."

"If I lived elsewhere it might," I concluded.

"You wouldn't reach as many people with your writings if you changed your name. People have come to trust your words. It'd be like starting all over to build that kind of loyal readership."

Punkin had fallen asleep guarding her prize ball and Rosie, having never dropped her watch, whisked it out of Punkin's limp grasp and raced across the room to place it beside Sally's hand. The game was on again.

I watched the action. "It wouldn't be wise to make a self-defeating business move," I expressed. "Soon I'll have seventeen books out under my name. You're right. It'd be a big mistake to try to change it now."

The fetch game was getting old and Sally distracted Rosie by asking the dogs if they wanted to go outside. The magic word incited a riot of barking and running feet. After they'd raced into the yard, she hid the ball on top of the refrigerator before going out the door to watch for the coyote.

While they were occupied, I restoked the fire embers and added a couple of pine logs. I lit a new cedar stick and freshened our drinks. Before we were seated again, Rosie was frantically searching for her ball. Her single-minded quest would keep her busy for quite some time.

∞ ∞ ∞

Baby curled up in Sally's lap, gave a deep sigh, and closed her eyes.

Pinecone and Punkin played tug of war with an old sock and Cheyenne settled herself beside my chair. Rosie, well, she was off in her own little world.

We watched the two pups at play. When Pinecone growled it made me laugh, for the sound was more like a windup toy than a real dog. As small as she was, she could hold her own in tugging games. Her persistence made up for her size.

Interest in the game waned early this autumn night. As though a whistle had blown to signal a time-out, both dogs left the sock in the middle of the room.

Punkin stretched out at my feet.

Pinecone jumped up on my lap, did a few testing circles in place, then settled down with nose tucked into my skirt.

To my surprise, Rosie was curled up on the hearth rug.

"Look on the hearth," I softly said to my friend.

She, too, was surprised that the Great Ball Quest had been abandoned so quickly. "They all crashed at the same time."

Now the only sounds heard were those of the crackling fire and the metered ticking of the pendulum wall clock.

Sounds of tranquillity.

Calming, mellow sounds that soothed the soul.

Seven, ten minutes passed in companionable silence as the wafting serenity was taken into our beingness. Rich moments like these were counted among the treasured blessings I cherished so much.

My friend whispered. "This is like meditating."

What a novel thought that was. Being immersed within the embracing atmosphere of warm tranquillity and absolute peacefulness was indeed exactly like experiencing the wonderful benefits of deep meditation.

"Yeah," I brightened, "that's very much what this feels like."

"This place is good for you. The Powers That Be knew what they were doing when they led you here. It's as though this valley has been waiting a long time for you to come home to it. And this cabin sat incomplete so you could incorporate your own finishing touches . . . put your own spirit essence into it."

I glanced about the cozy room and realized she was right. The ceiling beam was full of hanging baskets and bundles of drying wildflowers and sage I'd picked. The carpet was the dark forest green I'd always envisioned one day being in my place. The amber firelight, now gaily dancing across the dark knotty-pine walls, reflected the luster of my labors of staining and varnishing each panel that we'd nailed in place. My eyes passed over the coat closet we framed in and finished.

I smiled. "We did a pretty good job on that closet, didn't we?"

Her return smile was one that displayed inner pleasure at my personal sense of accomplishment. "Yes, we did. You'd never know it wasn't part of the original wall. We did all right for not being professional carpenters."

"My bedroom was a lot of work," I commented, thinking of the twelve-foot ceiling and the angled walls we'd paneled.

"And now it's completely you. It even looks like you, right down to the carved-oak cedar chest beneath your dormer window and the bookcase in the corner with all the children's picture books and old-fashioned dolls."

"Yeah, it is me. It has a good feel to it, too. But now we need to start on finishing your room."

Her palms shot up in a halting signal. "Oh no, we have all the time in the world for that project. I've got to focus on these paintings for *Star Babies*. These are *oil* paintings, Mary; you've no idea how long these are going to take. Besides," she added, "we ran out of paneling, remember? It's going to take us a long time to save up for enough raw paneling to finish out my room. It can wait." Her voice softened. "Mary, I felt we had to get your room done. I knew it was very important. You needed it done so you could personally feel at home here, more settled. I felt you needed at least one finished room to provide complete solace for you."

"You psychic or something?"

Her head shook. "Yeah, right."

"Well, I have to admit that all that raw drywall everywhere didn't exactly contribute to a solid 'settled' feeling, yet look at all we've managed to accomplish since moving in. We've paneled the entire downstairs and the upstairs bathroom and my room. We built the deck and fenced in a large yard for the dogs. We cut firewood for the winter and installed lighting fixtures throughout the house. We did plumbing. That pedestal bathroom sink was not a piece of cake to install. Gosh," I exclaimed, "we've managed to get a lot done, haven't we."

"We'll get it all done. In time."

And that struck me as humorous. "Oh, I think it'll be a long time before we run out of house projects to do. Actually," I mused, "I like the idea of working and puttering around the cabin. I enjoy being busy with it."

"Being busy with it is how you'll keep adding more and more of yourself into it."

"Yes!" I beamed with new ideas flowing forth in a sudden flood of visuals. "Maybe next spring we can build an arbor over the gate like we did at the stone cabin and, this time, I'll be here long enough to see the clematis cover it. Morning glories on the fences. And we could make another walkway out of log rounds. I really liked the rustic look of that."

My friend was grinning from ear to ear. She enjoyed playing in the dirt as much as I did. Though it was hard work, we'd managed to dig out a sloping hillside and install nine railroad-tie steps that led down into the lower yard area. We'd also planted a couple of young Rocky Mountain maples and had plans to add more around the cabin each spring. Since moving out West over twenty years ago, I'd missed the fall brilliance of the sugar and silver maples I'd grown up loving. I was thrilled beyond words when Sally brought two of them home from the nursery.

I voiced a thought. "It's so peaceful here, working on the landscaping is almost like a meditation, too."

She agreed with that. Then, "Whatever happened to that meditation book you were working on back in the stone cabin?"

"That was just prior to the archangel dream. It fell by the wayside after I realized I needed to write about the dream's message and then the *Star Babies* idea was also occupying my thoughts."

"Are you going to finish it? The meditation book?"

I immediately shook my head. "No. I'd been going for simplicity with it and I'd managed it so well that I came to realize that there weren't enough words to fill a whole book's worth . . . maybe a pamphlet, but certainly not a whole book. I looked over my outline chapters and saw that a few choice paragraphs on each subject were all that was needed. For instance, the beginning chapter was titled *No Assembly Required* and was basically an overview that said meditation is not a complex procedure. No parts or tools needed. No complicated steps."

"Really? You mean to tell me that you really didn't have enough material to do a book?"

"No, I didn't."

"Tell me about what you had."

"Why?"

"Well, your first chapter title makes me think you were doing the book with some humor and I'd like to hear more. *No Assembly Required.* How'd you come up with that? It's cute."

"I wasn't specifically going for humor or cute. The chapter headings just came out that way, but the text was all technical simplicity. I took the concepts and reduced them down to a simple, basic formula of words rather than scientific symbols. As to that title, how could I not come up with it? Meditation requires no assembly. You can't get clearer, simpler than that." I cracked a grin. "I agree that it's a bit humorous, but it also expressed my point."

"What about all the 'tools' and 'parts' people think they need? Did you go into those?"

"That was chapter two, *Bell, Book and Candle.* I'd explained that things such as music, incense, maintaining a rigid body position, etc., were *personal* elements one could add if they so chose. These were individualized enhancements only. They were never a necessary or integral aspect to achieving real meditation, and oftentimes served to hamper it. This chapter dealt with all the matters of inconsequence people connected with meditation."

"You didn't have enough to fill a chapter?"

"No. Once I said you didn't need all those extra parts of fluff and puff; what more was there to say about it?"

My friend thought on that. "What else? What was the next chapter?"

"*Of God and Gurus* . . . knowing the difference. This facet of meditation messes folks up big time. They think they need to follow some guru's specific methodology. Chant. Endure a cramped lotus position. Repeat a special mantra. While all of these elements are okay for a select few, they certainly are a hindrance for many others.

"Meditation is going Within yourself, reaching and touching the beautiful core of your beingness, where the essence of God resides. It's visiting a well and filling up with God's peacefulness and warmth of unconditional love. The Within has everything to do with God and nothing at all to do with gurus or any of their specialized meditative methodologies."

"What else?"

I grinned at her with a questioning look. "What, I'm supposed to go through the whole book now? Right now?"

"You got a hot date waiting at the door?"

Now I shot her a look of caution. "You're being a smart-mouth."

"Sue me," she quipped. "Seriously, I think this is interesting. And if you don't mind, I'd like to hear the rest of what you had planned for the book."

"Okay," I relented. "The next chapter was inspired by a real bugaboo of mine. It was called *Mistaken Identity* and addressed the fact that people are continually confusing meditation with contemplation. One is *passive,* where the mind is at rest with *nonthought* and the other is an *active* mind that *thinks* deeply on a specific idea. It is literally impossible to meditate on one's navel, or on nature, or on anything at all because meditation is nonthought. Whenever I'm in a bookstore and spy a book that's filled with sayings or philosophical ideas to 'meditate on' I cringe. These are books filled with ideas or visuals to *contemplate* on. They are meant to inspire active thought. To claim a book is a 'Meditation on this,' or a 'Meditations of someone' is a misnomer of theory . . . a contradiction in terms. It is an impossibility. My *Whispered Wisdom* book was meant to inspire contemplation in others through my own contemplative thoughts. To *think* is mind in an *active* state. That's contemplation. Meditation is mind in nonthought . . . passive.

"The next chapter I had outlined," I sheepishly grinned, "was called *A Glandular Thing*, and addressed the technical physiological workings of meditation—the glandular side. I'd pretty much reiterated the process I'd already covered in *Earthway*. I felt I was being redundant by going over it again."

"But this is different," she disagreed. "This was going to be an entire book devoted to meditation. Why would that seem repetitive to you?"

I lifted my shoulders. "It just did. This was something I'd already explained in full and I felt I was just filling another book with repeat information. I never want to do that, you know. I don't write books to write books . . . fill pages, if you know what I mean."

She rolled her eyes to the ceiling. "I hardly think you could ever be accused of that. You've always had different messages to convey. Still, a book devoted to one subject such as meditation would, by its very nature, include all you've previously had to say on it. I certainly don't view that as being redundant or being an author trying to fill pages."

"I do and I can't get past it. Anyway, the next planned chapter heading was *Quantum Meditation* and gave a glimpse into the vast expanse of universal reality in all its multidimensional forms. This was a simplistic composite view based on my own experiences coupled with all those advanced physics books I'd recently plowed through.

"The following chapter title was *The Ultimate High* and took folks into the experience of *virtual* meditation. That was kind of fun doing," I admitted with a playful smile.

"The final chapter was called *I Can't Meditate and Other Nonsensical Notions*. This one blew apart people's excuses for claiming they couldn't meditate. I added a last section to the book that had the long heading of *Confusing Conundrums and Their Simple Solutions*."

"Let me guess," Sally said. "This was a question-and-answer section based on your readers' letters."

"Yes. That's what it was going to be before I determined the book would be redundant and I decided against doing it. Honestly, after I got into it, there just was no elaboration or expanding to be done. Once all the bottom lines were stated in simple terms, each chapter would've ended up being no more than a few very well-worded paragraphs. I found myself trying to write The Book That Wasn't."

"Well, you have to go with your feelings. Still," she tried, "it could be a *little* book." An impish grin brightened her face. "You could call it *The Little Meditation Book* or *Rain's Little Book on Meditation*."

"Now you're being a smart-mouth and ridiculous. Besides, nobody calls me 'Rain' except you. It's not going to happen. I'd feel as though I were trying to *make* another title to add to my list–force one into existence. I can't do that."

"It wouldn't look like that at all."

"It'd feel like that. It'd feel like that to me."

"Then it's not going to happen, is it?"

"No."

"Yet," she commented, sounding like a diligent advocate for my readers, "with all the dozens of books out on meditation and the hundreds of classes, and zillions of teachers, people are still having trouble with it."

"I know. I know that."

"So . . . why not . . . ? Never mind."

"So . . . why not give it another shot?" I finished.

"Something like that."

"It's not only how I feel about doing it, it's also the evidence of people still having trouble with it. Why is that, do you think? How can that be when, as you say, there're 'dozens' of books, 'hundreds' of classes, and 'zillions' of teachers showing the ways of it?"

On Sally's lap, Baby twitched and barked in her sleep. She calmed with a few gentle strokes down her back.

She saw my point. "Simplifying something doesn't necessarily result in participation or instill the desire for same," she concluded. "Excuses will be readjusted, be more creative."

Her statement was right on target. It wasn't so much people having trouble with it as people *convincing* themselves they had trouble. I'd seen meditation be a two-sided coin, one that could pit ideology against commitment. Desire against theory. Passing fancy or frivolity versus a solid way of life. Those who took it lightly found excuses for their failure. Those who were committed to it because of a solid belief in it, succeeded. And one more book wouldn't make a bit of difference to either one.

"There's something interesting here," I noted. "If one's belief in an ideology, theory, or theological tenet is unshakable, their degree of commitment to it is very strong. Yet there are also those who depend on that act of commitment to keep a belief strong and alive to thrive."

"Sounds like choosing which came first, the chicken or egg."

"Yes. Well, that one is specifically determined by the evolutionist or the creationist, depending on which one answers. A person who is committed *because* of strong beliefs will do far better in life than the individual who depends on commitment to support beliefs. A case in point would be a good friend of mine who spent his childhood experiencing so-called paranormal events and UFO incidents. He naturally accepted these events as normal facts of life. They were reality . . . until he became romantically involved with a confirmed skeptic who *believed* she based her world view on science. I watched this young man emphatically deny all he'd experienced in deference to her beliefs. I watched him reject it all. This guy believes his young woman to be the epitome of intelligence and reason, yet they are barely over voting age. In lieu of appearing foolish or even crazy in her eyes, he forced himself into denial. He even avoids me now because I represent far-reaching concepts and, therefore, just maybe, I'm a little bit nutso for believing in my own experiences. How sad I feel for him. He let blossoming ego and ignorance wipe out his beautiful beliefs and erase all his experiences from the past. His beliefs were not strong enough to survive the first opposition they bumped into. He denies everything he's seen. He has no faith in self, no confidence in his sense of unique individuality. He now feels the need to conform to all that *she* is in order to feel secure in their relationship."

"That's similar to peer pressure," Sally observed, "yet that too wouldn't exist if confidence in one's individuality was strong."

"Mmmm. One's beliefs are a large portion of his or her unique identity. To deny those beliefs in deference to another's is to deny part of self. Confidence and commitment to beliefs can be easily shattered if the strength of those beliefs isn't strong, and nothing shatters that strength of conviction faster than ego, meaning the need to be accepted by others."

"Conformity. Forsaking beliefs to gain acceptance. That's going against the natural self. It's a forcing of one's nature into a foreign mold," Sally said.

"Yes. It exposes a fear of being different, a fear of expressing alternate ideas or diverse thought. It robs an individual of her or his beautiful uniqueness. In the end it says, 'I'm afraid to be me.' These two young people remind me of teenagers who know they have all life's answers. They know everything."

Sally repositioned Baby on her lap. "Your friend, later in life he's going to have real psychological problems if he keeps denying the reality of his past experiences. Right now he's avoiding you because you represent the reality of those same experiences he's trying to keep buried. You cause him inner conflict that he doesn't want to deal with."

"That's true. He also will never know self . . . what self thinks and believes. He can't know this because he is always believing in what others believe in order to be like them and accepted.

"I have some excellent books written by Nobel-laureate scientists and high-ranking government people that I'd love to give to his girlfriend to read. I haven't done so because I'm not sure it's the right approach."

"Are you concerned that you'd be interfering?"

"There is that possibility, yet something keeps prompting me to leave the situation alone."

"Maybe you just don't want to get involved."

I shook my head. "It's more than that, something having more depth than that." I looked down at the little pups asleep on my lap and stroked their silky heads. "There was a time in my life when I was fired up. The flames within me flared and roared to get the spiritual message out to everyone I could possibly reach." I chuckled. "If I were a woodstove I would've been blazing at 900 degrees and had the flue pipe glowing red hot. But now I'm doing a steady burn at a comfortable 300 degrees, a mellow fire that maintains an evenness, yet still crackles with sparks of life."

My words turned both our heads toward the woodstove logs that were flaring their glowing colors of orange and red.

"With all I've been through in the past four years, I've been left with a deep mellowness that tempered the raging fire I once had. That new mellowness is a profound acceptance of life, of how others believe and behave. The vigilance of my work has become passive; not less, just softer and . . . ."

"It's matured," she defined. "It's a result of your recent transition, evolution. You no longer get into those animated and impassioned outrages over injustices. Now you calmly look at them, contemplate a bit, then pray over them." She laughed. "Just look at the recent instances where I got upset over some life incident or someone's behavior and you'd tell me to calm down and accept. A year ago you would've been just as outraged as I was. Mary, you've mellowed out, you really have."

The firelight reflected her smile back to me. "The tempest of your spiritual youth–the raging whitewater river–has transformed itself into a clear mountain stream."

"Oh my," I exclaimed, "that was colorful. Maybe you should write books too."

"What would I write? *Living With Summer Rain*? I don't think so. My analogy just came from being around you so much; besides, I don't write–I paint. Anyway, my point is that you're different than you were before. The Picasso has turned into a Rembrandt."

"Michelangelo," I corrected.

Her brow rose in an unspoken question.

"We share more," I clarified. "His work was very spiritual," I said, getting up from the chair.

I took a pillow off the love seat and stretched out on the carpet before the woodstove.

Pinecone liked that idea and her tiny feet traversed the length of my spine. With a baby's-breath sigh, she settled comfortably on the small of my back. She was as light as a feather.

Punkin Pie curled up beside me.

Facing the raised hearthstone, I was nearly eye to eye with Rosie, who was too drowsy to do more than acknowledge my presence through half-opened lids.

I bunched the pillow beneath my chin. "Getting back to my friend," I said, realizing that we'd gone from meditation to commitment to acceptance, "I feel the need to let it be. Maybe he needs to come to some breakthrough realizations on his own, maybe mature more. I think any prompting from me at this stage would only serve to heighten his current resolve."

"Like a teenager who becomes determined to do something forbidden the more a parent says not to."

"Exactly. He needs to mature beyond adolescent behavior and thought."

"But Mary, he's old enough to know better."

"Since when is immaturity confined to an age limit?"

"You made your point."

∞ ∞ ∞

"So," I said, "we got here from the subject of meditation and why I'm not doing the book. Let's go back to meditation, or did you have another subject in mind?"

"Meditation's fine."

I eased Pinecone off my back and sat cross-legged before the fire.

She tiptoed over my folded legs to nestle down in my lap.

"Deep meditation," I began, "very deep meditation is open ended. It's a corridor that leads to an opened door at the other end." My mouth formed a crooked smile of frustration. "Some concepts are difficult to explain in easily understood terms, so I'm going to have to equate them to recognized visuals to help clarify what I'm talking about here.

"The deepest state of meditation brings one through this opened doorway or portal. It would be like walking down a spaceship passageway and then floating out an opened door or portal into deep space. This deep space element of the universe or consciousness is what I call *quantum meditation*. It's the state of deepest *place* one can go during meditation. It's a specific vibratory *frequency* one attains. And, because it's a quantum state of reality, destinations are endless. The limitless realities that exist are like passing through layer after fine layer of diaphanous onion skin." I paused out of uncertainty. "I'm not sure I'm explaining this quantum idea clearly enough."

"I think you are. From what you said, I got the idea that there are no final destinations within this quantum meditation state—no dead-end roads. It would be like believing Woodland Park was as far as you could travel, then once arriving there, you realize there's more beyond and you travel down to Colorado Springs, believing that that's the end of the world, but then you realize Denver's beyond that. On and on like the cities being the onion-skin layers you pass through—each layer being a different possible destination."

I brightened. "Yes! Each layer being a finer frequency of reality, a whole different world, so to speak.

Each world feeling as three-dimensional and real as this one. And the tactile *feel* to these is what I call *virtual meditation*."

Sally wanted to express her understanding so far. "*Quantum* meditation refers to the vast and limitless dimensional *locales*. *Virtual* meditation refers to the experiential *feel* of them."

"That's it! I want to say that the *virtual* aspect is like doing that computer game thing, you know, where you put some sort of contraption on your head and it's supposed to make you feel as though you're right there in the scene. But using that crude example only diminishes the actual sensual and tactile extent of what's really felt. When you're in the *quantum* meditative state, the *virtual* reality of all sensations such as touch, smell, hearing, and sight is greatly magnified and enhanced. The intensity of color; the sharpness and clarity of visuals is vibrant, almost alive!" I suppose my excitement was showing, for my friend began grinning as I became more and more animated.

"But, Sally, it's so incredible! What's out there is so . . . So . . . ."

"Real?" she finished.

"Yes! So *real*! So real and alive that it makes the third dimension feel like it's in a fog, a primitive state of existence that lacks clarity. What's so fascinating about experiencing *virtual* meditation is that you're really there. Your total mind is there. Which," I reminded, "is why you have to be in complete nonthought for meditation."

I saw a frown flicker across my friend's face. "You just said . . . ."

"I know. It sounded contradictory to my ears, too. I need to clarify this better. Mmmm," I mused. "Let's go all the way back to the beginning again.

"Meditation is a state of complete physiological and mental rest. You're going to meditate, so you rest your body in a relaxed position. You close your eyes and begin to breathe easy. No active mental attention or focus is given to stray thoughts that wander through the mind. These merely mosey in and back out—just passing through.

"Once all the thoughts have gone on their way, the mind is left with nonthought. Mind at rest. Soon all sense of self has evaporated. No spatial reference exists. No sense of body is felt. This is the point where one begins moving along the passageway or corridor toward the opened doorway ahead. Remember though, and this is important, you're not *there* if you *notice* this corridor or say to yourself, 'Oh cool! I'm in the corridor!' because you've already checked your coat (consciousness) at the *beginning* of this corridor. What you *do* carry with you is your mind at rest—the pure *mind*. The longer amount of time this mind-at-rest state is maintained, the deeper you'll move into true meditation; you're there when you begin to float out the portal into the vastness of *quantum* meditation. Here is where only mind exists. Only the pure mind holds you there. One *conscious* thought will snap you back to your chair or couch. Yet this is a rarity if you're really there, because all sense of separate beingness has been long gone. It's a prerequisite, so to speak.

"So, now the *mind* has reached a *quantum* meditation locale. The mind experiences so much more without its hampering body that dulls exquisite sensations such as taste, touch, and sight. Now the *mind* does the touching and seeing. Now the *mind* experiences *virtual* meditation."

"I see," she said, "that helped define the difference between being *conscious* of the self's own beingness and the existence and experience of pure mind consciousness without self attached."

We were silent for a while after that. This wasn't due to having nothing to say, but rather seemed to be a natural pause brought on by the room's natural homey atmosphere. Taking some quiet moments to enjoy the cabin's soothing ambiance was a good part of what made these impromptu evening conversations so companionable.

The aspen burned with a steady flame.

Pitch in the pine logs crackled and sizzled.

Over the paneled walls, reflections of the woodstove's firelight danced with those of the glowing candles.

Scent of cedar meandered lazily around the room, fragile blue tendrils swirled and floated on warm air currents.

Sally joined her voice with those of the ticking clock and crackling fire. "Within these symbolic onionskin layers of *quantum* meditation locales, is one of the layers a reflection of earth?"

Before I could respond, she adjusted the wording of her question.

"No, wait a minute. I don't mean to say 'reflection' because that would represent a mirrored image. Parallel, that's what I'm getting at. Is one of the layers a parallel universe?"

"Interesting question. Yes. Each dimensional or frequency layer is a different reality unto itself. One is a near-parallel of earth."

"Near? Not exact?"

"Only in the sense of who it's peopled with. Let me try to explain. Okay, say I'm meditating right now. I've reached the stage where all sensation and awareness of self has dropped away—I've left consciousness behind. I'm moving out through the layers of *quantum* meditation and find the parallel universe to be the mind's destination. I'm now also in *virtual* meditation, where the pure mind experiences everything the physical body and consciousness does in the waking third dimension state. Are you following me?"

She nodded. "Yes. Though you're in the *quantum* meditation location of a parallel earth, through the mind's ability to experience *virtual* meditation, you *feel* as real as if you were back on earth."

"Yes. That's because it *is* just as real, except for the greatly heightened senses I mentioned before. On this parallel earth, all geographic and physiological elements are the same—replicated. Every tree, stone, and blade of grass is there. Your house in your neighborhood. Your pets, your car, your friends and family."

"You said the people are what makes it a little different."

"Yes, I was getting to that. The people living in the three-dimensional earth are duplicated in the quantum parallel earth, but here there are additional people who do not live on the physical earth."

My friend frowned.

I did too. "I'm not doing a very good job of explaining this, am I? Okay, let's go back to my example. I'm in deep meditation and my mind went to the parallel earth realm. Mind is now experiencing *virtual* meditation. Our cabin is there. It's there with all the work we've recently done to it. Your Toyota is parked out the back gate. It happens to be early morning. You're asleep in your room and Baby is curled up at your feet. I tiptoe down the stairs, out of the house, and drive away. I follow down and around the same roads I routinely traveled a long time ago. I park the car in front of my old teacher's cabin, race up her steps and fling open the door. Her toothless grin beams at me!"

Sally's jaw dropped. "But she's . . . ."

My smile widened like a clown's. "She's *there*! Mind never dies! It controls matter over there! Since the spirit is the mind's total consciousness, she can manifest a physical form to interact with at the Parallel Quantum location!"

"Look!" she exclaimed, holding out her arm for me to see. "That gave me major goose bumps!"

I laughed. "Discovering the vast extent of universal physics can do that."

She shuddered as if to shake off the creepy sensations. "Let me think about this for a minute."

"Okay."

I turned my gaze to the glowing fire embers and waited for her highly analytical mind to whip through its process with its usual computer speed to make the one concluding realization. I grinned when I heard her responsive stroke of genius.

"Shit!" she excitedly spat out. "*Shit!* That means you can go there and spend consecutive days with her! That means, if this *quantum* locale is just like here, nothing has changed from *before* . . . except the vehicle you drive there with and the house you leave from."

"Probably."

"Probably?" That one word was full of recognized meaning. "You haven't been there in years, have you. You don't go there."

"No. I've no reason to. My work is here in this reality. She's in my heart."

She thought on that. "So that was just an example you gave . . . about you driving out there by way of meditation."

"Yes, an example of the parallel-earth reality of the meditative *quantum* locale."

"And," she added, "all events the *mind's* pure consciousness experiences there through *virtual* meditation are just as real as experiencing them here in the physical conscious state."

"More real," I emphasized. "More intense."

Sally was pensive again. "Your teacher wouldn't be there for anyone else, would she."

"No. First of all, someone would have to *virtually* travel to the cabin's precise location. They'd need to know the way. Then they'd find it deserted."

"Why?"

"Because she'd said I was her last. That meant for all realities."

"But you have gone there in your meditations and seen her—communicated with her like before."

"Yes. Many years ago. Not since then. My work is here."

"She advised you to stay here?"

"Not in so many words. I had a spiritual evolution to go through. I needed a solid three-dimensional focus. When I went into *quantum* meditation I went to other levels—different realities. I won't return to her parallel cabin until the time is right. I'll know when that will be because it'll happen naturally—without prior thought or notice."

Those words brought her to a related thought. "Were you in *quantum* when you had the archangel visitation?"

"Yes, but his brightness brought my mind back to consciousness through a physical sensation of my three-dimensional beingness and I believe it pulled me back down to a conscious subsurface level—a dream state."

"You sure you ended up in the dream state?"

"No, I'm not absolutely sure. I'm not sure because of where the dogs were when I awoke. They were in the same place they were when the 'dream' ended. And the room, the room had a specific feel to it

. . . as though some subtle residual element were left of his essence."

"Like the faint lingering scent of someone's perfume after they've passed through a room."

"Yes, something like that."

"So even in *quantum* meditation, the mind has experiences–*virtual* experiences–and thought. The mind is active."

"Active with conscious thought evidenced in the *quantum* dimension. Mind having no attendance to the three-dimensional body or earthly-related events, only those it *virtually* experiences as generated through its own pure thought.

"The pure mind manifests a desired physical form to have the experiences in, just like one dreams of him or herself in a body. Only, in *quantum* locales, there is no surrealism, confusion, or symbology that dreams contain. In *quantum* locales and realities everything appears as solid and as real as here. All experiences have logic and natural sequence. And that's another reason I know the entire archangel visitation didn't take place in *quantum*–it was illogical that I never had to refuel the woodstove. The same logs held their flames without being consumed. That wouldn't happen if I'd been in my parallel earth cabin."

"Maybe the archangel kept them burning," she tried, "so you wouldn't have to interrupt the flow of conversation."

My brow shot up. "I still got out of the chair to keep checking on it, didn't I? No, it was the one idiosyncrasy that led me to believe he came in a dream state."

"Then what of the feel to the room when you returned to full consciousness? What of the placement of the dogs?"

My palms upturned with that. "I never said I had all the answers, only God has those. All I can go by are my own experiences and take note of their subtle nuances. There are times, like the archangel event, when the elements don't fit prior experiences. Though I don't always have a pat, definitive explanation for those, I'm left recounting them precisely as they happened . . . with or without a positive I.D. of the technicality."

"Well," she sighed, "I still think you have enough information for that meditation book."

"I don't."

"Obviously you believe that, but what you've just said about the *quantum* meditation realities and the mind's *virtual* meditative experiences was fascinating. You could take it further to expand on the other *quantum* places; you know, all those other onion-skin layers."

"Expand?"

"No? No expanding, huh?"

"Huh. People need to keep their minds on the here and now. The archangel's message made that crystal clear. Pay attention to today. Be aware. Make behavioral choices. *Carpe diem.*"

Her expression was serious. "Seize the day. I see your point when you put it like that. Why would he give you his message to pass on if he saw you were going to distract people with other realities?"

"Exactly."

Seeming deep in thought, my friend had paused.

"What are you thinking?" I asked.

"I was thinking about the part of the archangel's message where he defined the three aspects of God. Actually," she admitted, "I've been giving it quite a lot of thought lately."

"Oh? How so?"

"Reader reaction . . . or," she corrected, "*over*reaction, the ease with which some will slide into delusional thought over it."

"There's always that element, isn't there? There always has been. People's ego will clench onto a new idea with a death grip and cast themselves as the star of it. Oh yes," I nodded, "you watch, false Shekinahs will be coming out of the walls. Delusional women will be scrambling to claim the title. They'll be proclaiming to be God's female aspect on earth, while others will think they're going to birth her."

Sally shook her head. "They won't realize that, by the very nature of their proclamation, they'll be discrediting their own claim."

"No, they won't consider that because the Shekinah's determined state of anonymity doesn't play into their desired notoriety or expectation of fame."

"Doesn't that kind of behavior bother you? I mean, it's got to hurt when you're trying so hard to bring some light into the world."

"Oh, I don't know, Sally. I've mellowed, remember? There was a time when I was younger and this type of behavior would've set me off into a ranting outrage that'd be more animated than a cartoon character, then I'd stew over it for weeks afterward." I gave a wry smile. "I was very impassioned about my work back then."

"Lady," she informed, "you may not think it, but you still are."

"Yes, but in a different way. The youthful impetuosity and hair-trigger response isn't there anymore. Now there's more contemplation and acceptance. Like now, I know the Shekinah is currently a grown woman living life securely wrapped in her anonymity. I also know there will be ego-driven women who will claim to be her or even birth her. I know this behavior is inevitable and I accept that. Yes," I pointed out, "having acceptance doesn't necessarily freeze or numb one's natural responses. I still feel a quiet spiritual nausea over certain behavior and claims, but the animated outrages I once reacted with are gone."

"I'm sorry," she said with some sadness in her voice. "I'm sorry you sometimes feel pain from people's response to your work, how your words get twisted and woven into altered concepts."

"Their response is not my responsibility. Every person is held accountable for what they do with information, spiritual or otherwise. Knowledge can lead to wisdom or folly, growth or retardation; it's all in how it's handled. I will tell you this though, any woman claiming to be the female aspect of God walks with her ego full-blown before her. The true Shekinah will be known by her light alone. No, don't be sorry for my feelings. My work is fulfilling because I take it seriously and am focused on doing what I'm here to do. That's more than enough. Since the archangel made me see that people's responses to the messages weren't my responsibility, much of the weighty burden I once carried has been lifted. Rather than being pained, I accept instead. Acceptance of people's behavior is far healthier than personalizing and internalizing it. Acceptance can be a beautifully liberating attitude—an uplifting way of life."

"Yes, but still, it doesn't numb the heart. You can still be hurt."

"Let's hope nothing ever numbs the heart. Sure, I can be hurt and affected by others. Having acceptance doesn't make me Stoneheart. Acceptance filters ignorance with wisdom, though. It becomes a powerful shield, a screen that tempers and softens the cruelty and ignorance that attempt to touch one's life."

"And does it also dull the pain of empathy?"

I hesitated with that. "No, nothing dulls true empathy."

∞ ∞ ∞

Sally didn't care for my heavier tone. "Let's go back to the meditation book. We got a little off track."

"Sure, whatever you want."

"Now that I have a wider view of your perspective on this meditation issue, I agree with you about not doing the book."

"Really."

"Really. The *quantum* and *virtual* chapters defeat the simplicity you were going for. You made the concepts easy enough to understand. You succeeded in doing that. But . . . well, you'd be showing them a yacht when most are only skilled enough to handle a rowboat."

Her words hit hard. "Dammit! You're right. That's exactly what I did. I was going to take it way too far. Instead of being satisfied with *praying* among the congregation, I inferred that they could be *conducting* the ceremony. I'd inadvertently had them trying to be astronauts instead of being content to admire the stars from the ground. Why didn't I see that?"

She grinned. "You have a tendency to get carried away."

I returned a sheepish expression. "Yeah, I know. Once I get going on something I tend to leave no stone unturned."

"That's usually a thorough way of explaining concepts. That's how your discourses get off onto so many interconnected aspects. Each stone you overturn is an associated element of the main issue and you go after it, address it."

"But," I interrupted, "some subject matters are better left to self-discovery. Some stones should only be overturned by the individual when he or she has progressed far enough to stumble upon them. I was going to set out a royal banquet instead of serving country meat and potatoes. Yeah," I chuckled, "my work is down-home, meat-and-potatoes style. How'd I get away from that?"

"Like I said, you tend to get carried away sometimes. This just happened to be one of them."

"It would've been a terrible mistake, you know. I would've done a disservice to those who are trying to meditate." I released a sigh. "For the most part, meditation is a huge success for folks if they can just find the time to rest their bodies for a while. Those who get to the nonthought stage are a huge success and greatly benefit from it. I'd be pleased to see folks getting that far with it. They don't need more to go within."

"You're berating yourself, Mary."

"No, I'm not. I'm just . . . ."

"Yes, you are. All you did with that planned book was share your knowledge and personal experience. You were being honest and straightforward. You exposed the entire universe rather than uncovering one star to focus on. It was too ambitious and overwhelming for the simplicity you were shooting for, that's all." She softly smiled. "You had all the bases loaded before the first ball was pitched."

My face scrunched up in question. "What?"

"Never mind," she laughed, remembering I didn't know beans about baseball. "All I'm trying to say is that you shouldn't berate yourself for sharing what you know."

"But I carried it too far."

"What, that's a sin? Cut yourself some slack, would

you? All you did was outline a book a bit too extensively, you never would've finished it that way."

"You don't think so?"

She shook her head. "Nope. You would've caught it eventually."

I envisioned myself developing the two offending chapters. I wouldn't have gotten far. "You're right. I would've caught it and then realized I had an even smaller book yet."

"So! Now that that's all settled, you can concentrate on your next book!"

Now it was my turn to shake my head. "Nuh-uh. It's not time. I'm feeling the need to stay open, leave a gap of free time between projects."

Her brows knitted together. "You didn't mention that before. What's going on?"

"I don't know yet. You've seen how these things go. Could be anything."

"You still getting flashes of that house?"

My friend was referring to mental visuals I'd been having of a very small sparsely furnished house. It seemed to be constructed of adobe or cement block. These visions left me with the impression that I lived there alone. The lack of personal items in the house gave off an essence of severe material apathy. I felt this place was in my future. Neither of us liked the feel of it, nor did we enjoy speculating on the possible reasons for it to become a future reality.

"No, not as often as I was before. I haven't had it in a while. I'm hoping the probability for it has altered."

"Well there's a reason why you need to suspend your book writing. Do you have a time frame for this hiatus?"

"No. I don't know how long."

"Well then? We take it one day at a time like

always and see what presents itself. I'm just glad you haven't had recent visuals of that house." A shiver rippled through her. "It sounded like a lonely place."

I shrugged. "Unfortunately, it did have that feel to it. I may utilize this open time to begin work on *Pinecones and Woodsmoke.* That'll be an ongoing work in progress that can keep me busy for several years. I can alternate work on that and projects with the cabin. It won't be like I'll have nothing to do. I still need to put the cedar panels up in my bedroom closet."

"As soon as we get paid again we can see about buying those. Getting paid every three months has made us experts at budgeting."

"Tell me about it. After Uncle Sam grabs his chunk off the top for my estimated taxes and money is put aside to cover the three house payments each quarter, we're lucky we've been able to manage all we have with this place."

"When you think about it, yeah. I mean, when we bought the place we were led to believe the existing generator was fine. We never figured on having to replace it."

I laughed at that. "Neither did we know it'd take four hundred a month in gasoline to fuel it!"

"We've no choice. That's our utility bill. Who in the world's got twenty-seven thousand dollars laying around to pay the power company to bring electricity down to the house? We sure don't. Few people would. I think it's a crime what they want to put power here, especially when it's right up the road. It should be everyone's right to have electricity like the government made it everyone's right to have access to a phone line. Well," she sighed, "we're getting along okay with the little generator."

"Still," I said, "it's been a real inconvenience for you to lug your computer over to Sindy's house every time we need to put one of my finished books on it."

"I'm okay with it, but that's nothing," she smiled, "what about our thirty-mile trips—one way—into town each week to do our laundry?"

The laughter was getting infectious. "Well, I tried, didn't I? I tried to work the washer in the basement."

"Oh yeah, you ended up bailing out the water with a coffee can and wringing out the clothes because the generator couldn't handle the washer pump. Clothes were spread all over the deck to dry. God, that was funny."

"Oh, it was just hilarious. At least I gave it a try. Well, it's a blessing the typewriter works off the generator. I blew the copy machine big time, but the typewriter works. I'm thankful for that."

One thing led to another. "It's kinda funny to think back on when we were first learning about all this, isn't it?"

I agreed with a widening smile. "Can't vacuum when the well pump's running. Can't use a portable phone at all because it won't hold a charge. Can't use an answering machine because the generator's off when we're not home. Can't use a toaster or microwave."

We were making a good joke of our present situation and laughing at it.

"Can't use the Mr. Coffee," Sally added, "got to do that old-time range-top percolator brewing. And here's the really fun one . . . can't flush a toilet without the generator running and . . . ."

"And sometimes we can't get it going!" I finished, laughing so hard that tears began to cloud my eyes. "Oh gosh, we're a mess, aren't we?" I wiped my eyes and lifted Pinecone up to cuddle her. Our frivolity had stirred the dogs and Cheyenne had come over to wash my happy tears.

"It's okay, Cheyenne," I soothed. "I'm fine, just being silly, is all."

Sally's solemn voice drew my attention. "Mary, we're going to be okay. We can laugh about it all but I know that the generator noise going all day bothers you sometimes and . . . ."

I shrugged my shoulders. "It's all right. I . . . ."

"I know you miss the quiet sounds. Wind through the trees. Birdsong. Just the silence sometimes. We won't always have a generator running. It'll just take time."

"I know. I'm doing good with it."

"You're managing. Managing is what you're doing." She broke into a smile. "This new mellow acceptance you've attained has come in handy."

I returned the smile. "Believe me, it's a blessing, a real blessing. I'm sure, a couple of years ago, all these little inconveniences would've kept me in a constant state of frustration; today they're just things to adjust to, find ways around. I'm okay, I really am. I wouldn't trade this place for anywhere. I love it here. Besides," I reminded, "I still get to hear the wind in the trees and birdsong when I'm writing out on the deck and you thoughtfully turn off the generator for a few hours."

She grinned with that. "You realize we're compromising the refrigerator food for birdsong when I do that, don't you? The refrigerator's off all night long."

"Oops."

She smirked. "I was only kidding you. That refrigerator holds the cold very well. It doesn't hurt anything to have it off for a couple of daylight hours."

"All in all," I concluded, "we've gotten so used to living this way that it's become a routine way of life. I really don't miss anything. Well," I reconsidered, "it would be nice to be able to use the washer and dryer and have your computer operable, but we manage fine despite those. This is still the best place I could be right now and I'm perfectly happy here."

"Until you're guided to be elsewhere."

"Well, sure, until then. But you know what?"

"Why do I have the feeling you're going to say something philosophical? What?"

"I've learned something here."

"*Some* thing?"

"A particular something. I learned the true meaning of the saying 'Home is where the heart is.' I came to Colorado over twenty years ago and believed I was 'looking' for a special piece of land to settle on, to call home. So much thought and energy was given to the idea of getting *settled* that it never dawned on me that I was 'settled' *wherever* I was."

"But," she added, "the heart has to be in that place. The heart isn't in it if you don't have that settled feeling about it."

"That's just it, isn't it? It's a choice. The heart *should* be in wherever destiny has you placed at any given point in time.

"Living the moment, remember? You miss so much of today when you're always stretching your neck to see what's beyond the horizon. That saying is backward. It should be *Heart is where the home is.* That means: *put* your heart into wherever you are! No matter where your home is, no matter how temporary it might be or seem, it's still *home* and your heart needs to be in it.

"Another aspect of this that came as a couple of questions I contemplated was: What is *settled?* and, Are we ever really settled? Pondering these two questions, I came to the conclusion that the idea of being settled is mostly an illusion, a matter of relativity.

"To begin with, if we're here in this body for a limited amount of time, in actuality, we're only *borrowing* these bodies for a while. Physical life is an intermittent state of being for our spirits. So, stepping way back, we see that being on this planet is temporary. The use of these bodies is temporary, so too are all the different dwellings we live in. Is there really such a state as 'settled' when, on the grand scale, nothing is permanent? We're biding our time in the most spiritual way we can. Each day we help as many people as opportunities present. We pay acute attention to our surroundings and give thanks for the blessings we recognize as such. We love. We love and, maybe, we're fortunate enough to be loved back. We honor God and practice goodness until our time here comes to an end and we move into the light to begin another temporary adventure." I smiled wide then. "*Settled* is when all your spirit's adventures and temporary dwellings come to a final close. Settled is being back with God."

"Do you *ever* give your mind a rest?"

"Of course," I beamed, "when I'm meditating! Well, gosh, Sally, there're a million things to contemplate. I could sit and spend my entire life thinking on . . . ."

"You'd get piles," she quipped.

I threw the dog ball at her and pandemonium broke out.

Rosie charged for it.

Punkin scampered after Rosie.

Pinecone and Baby barked.

And Cheyenne tried to doggie-discipline them all.

"I'm letting them outside," I said, getting up off

the floor. As I entered the kitchen with five dogs racing past my feet, the ball bounced off my back.

"I'll get the fire and generator," Slugger called.

I didn't bother grabbing the gun on the way out because the coyote seemed wary of Cheyenne. She was the protector of the little ones. Thing was, Cheyenne didn't always go out with the Yorkies. I also didn't flip on the yard lights before walking out, because the mountainside was already aglow with silver moonlight.

The dogs chased one another down the railroad-tie steps while I strolled about the upper yard.

Sally was beneath the front porch and I heard the generator engine wind down.

Silence. Oh, how preciously sweet it was to my ears.

A gentle breeze tickled the aspen leaves. Their responsive whispered giggles were music to my soul. I closed my eyes and soaked up the peacefulness of the woodland night. I sighed and then smiled back at the winking stars. I felt so blessed. So happy. So complete.

The engine noise shattered the fragile, crystal night. Sally had filled the generator and had it going again.

I reluctantly turned away from the forest. "C'mon, doggies!" I called. "Time to go in!"

Everyone came running. Everyone but Rosie.

"Rosie!" I called.

No Rosie.

"ROSIE! You get up here before the Bogey Coyote gets you!"

She beelined it up the steps two at a time and skidded around the opened door on two legs.

Cheyenne properly dog-chastised her for not coming when she was called. It seemed that Cheyenne had appointed herself as mother of all the dogs. At least that's how it appeared to me because, whenever they're disciplined, Cheyenne always gets in their face with the last word, "Arf!" On the other hand, she protects them like a mother bear with cubs. There'd been a few times when Cheyenne barked ferociously at Sally or me while we scolded one of the little ones. That didn't go over too well with either of us. At any rate, there's a heck of a lot of love between these 'little people' of the house. In one way or another, it's always showing. Their vibrant personalities are all so uniquely different that they're very much like having small children in the house.

Rosie is the Dennis the Menace. Pinecone, the little pixie who loves to lick and lick her kisses for you. Punkin Pie, the Bumbler who follows me everywhere and is overflowing with affection. Cheyenne, my personal security force and surrogate Yorkie mother. And Baby, the refined real Yorkie mother who I call Queen Mother, who doesn't let Sally out of her sight. All of them so precious, so loving . . . more blessings to treasure.

∞ ∞ ∞

After the dogs had been re-energized by the fresh alpine air, their dynamos were roaring at full power.

Sally and I returned to our respective places and watched their playful antics. Of course, Queen Mother never cared much for childish ways–too undignified–so she curled into Sally's lap to oversee the wild activity of her offspring.

Ten minutes passed.

My friend noticed that, while my eyes were following the raucous action of the pups, my mind was clearly elsewhere.

"What're you thinking about?" she asked.

"Ohhh, stuff," came the obscure reply.

"That usually means you don't think it's important enough to talk about."

I shrugged. "Usually."

She didn't push.

Her statement drew a comment from me. "It's amazing how many thoughts a person can have in one day; most being superficial, not substantial enough to support conversation."

"The mind goes practically nonstop all day. That's why it gets irrational and dysfunctions without the rest period sleep gives it. Sleep deprivation short-circuits the mind's physiological housing. I take it you were having one or more superficial thoughts."

"Mmmm, more like an initial one leading into another and another."

"You do a lot of that."

"All of life is related in some way." I smiled. "Interconnectedness. The great Web of Life."

"So what were you thinking about?" she finally inquired.

I rose from the chair, went to my desk, and returned to the living room. "Let me read you something."

Sitting cross-legged before the woodstove, I adjusted the granny glasses on my nose and set the seven-pound dictionary on the raised hearth. Using the amber firelight for illumination, I began searching. After finding what I was looking for, I rested my left hand on the page and flipped a major part of the book over on it to search for a second word. Finding it, I said, "I want to read you the definitions of two words." Starting with the second word I had located in the back third of the book, I read, ". . . *a specific fundamental set of beliefs and practices as agreed upon by a number of persons or sects.*" I glanced over at my friend. "Want me to repeat it?"

"No. Go on."

I then flipped back the massive center section of pages. The book was now opened to where I'd held the place with my hand. I read the definition for the first term I'd looked up. "'*a particular system of religious worship with its rites and ceremonies as venerated by a group or sect.*' Did you get that?"

"Got it."

I gently closed the book. Leaving it on the warm hearth, I turned to face Sally. Before I could say anything further, she commented, "Obviously you've read the same definition for two synonyms."

My brow rose. "Obviously?"

"Yes."

"So you'd say that both these words meant the same thing."

"Sure. Am I supposed to guess the words?"

"My intent wasn't to make a guessing game out of it. My intent was to make a point. The two words are 'cult' and 'religion.'"

Surprise lit up her face. "What prompted this bit of research?"

"It was Wednesday, when we stopped in the casino to drop off a signed book for Steve and we played a little nickel video poker."

"You do heavy thinking while playing poker, do you?"

"Sure, don't you? It doesn't take a rocket scientist to play that. Anyway, I was playing and also watching the news on the television. They were reporting on some 'cult' and I couldn't understand why they were repeatedly using that specific term when the group was a spiritually based one. The indiscriminant use of that word began to irritate me. It was getting worn out. I was tired of hearing it from newspeople every time I turned around. And from what I was hearing about this particular group, I could discern nothing more sinister about them than their having specific religious beliefs.

"That got me thinking. If this were a religious group, why didn't the newspeople say that—use those terms—instead of calling them a cult? I didn't see why these people warranted a 'cult' distinction. It sounded like an effective method of branding a group of spiritual people or demeaning their beliefs. The cult word prejudiced the general public against a group on a national scale when it was used so loosely on television. It's no longer used accurately . . . or so it appeared to me.

"So as I sat playing, I wondered why these newspeople prejudiced the public against this group by calling them a cult instead of a religious sect, when all they did was stage a mild protest. I wondered what criteria were used by newspeople to determine their choice of words when describing or labeling others. They had a responsibility to be accurate and maybe it was I who didn't understand the distinction. When we got back home, I looked up 'cult' and 'religion' . . . the Catholic Church could be considered a cult. Fundamentalist radical groups aren't even referred to as cults, so what's the deal here?"

Sally had some input on this. "It's a prejudicial attitude toward any individual or group having beliefs that are considered anything remotely outside the realm of the established norm, especially those related to spiritual aspects."

"Who determined that norm?" I asked, "some news reporter who writes the TV script for the anchor to read? I don't see any logic applied. I've heard the Indian's Peyote Church referred to as both a peyote cult and a peyote religion. A group of people believing in a different concept does not make them a cult.

That's discriminating against free thought. It's giving the wrong message . . . a nasty message. It demeans one's right to express his or her unique individuality. It stunts societal growth by leaning toward an intolerant attitude."

"I wouldn't disagree with you on any of those points. It's a judgmental and prejudicial term, yet that's also the way of it. What can you do?"

I sighed. "Go out and shake people."

That amused my friend. "You what?"

"I know that must sound funny coming from me. Highly uncharacteristic. Yet there are times I feel like running out and getting in humanity's face. Show them how their behavior and choice of terminology are serving to perpetuate prejudice."

Sally suppressed a grin. "I can build you a soapbox."

"Oh, cute. That was real cute. And I'd look like a fruitcake, too."

"Wait a minute. You wouldn't have to look like a raving lunatic. You could give talks. Didn't you entertain the idea of doing something like that a few years ago? You called it . . . I can't remember what you called it."

"Communion. I called my hypothetical talks 'communion' because I would've been 'communing' *with* people, not 'talking' *at* them."

The firelight caught the new sparkle in her eyes. "Well?"

"Well, what?"

"Go commune!"

"Wrong. There's another side to that. Getting out there to commune puts me smack dab in the public eye." I shook my finger in warning. "That's a no-no. It goes against the grain."

"What grain?"

"The fabric of my beingness. My principles."

"But you still feel like running out and shaking people, getting in their faces."

"On the rare occasion, yes."

"You've put yourself in a Catch-22, you know."

"No, I haven't. Humanity has."

"You both have. It's humanity's behavior that pulls you to go out there. It's your own principles that hold you back."

"Touché, my friend. Touché."

"You're not left without recourse, though. Why don't you write a book covering these things? A book covering subjects like prejudicial attitudes and speech, the psychological behavioral mechanisms that continue to harm society?"

"Another book."

"Why not, if you've something else important to convey?"

"Sally, I never want to come across as being someone who's lecturing."

"Bad behavior warrants a lecture. At the very least it needs someone who brings attention to it. When your girls were little, didn't you bring their attention to bad behavior? Teach them the difference between impolite and proper social behavior?"

"Now you're talking about a parent's responsibility toward rearing children."

"I'm talking about bad behavior. Behavior that harms others. I'm not making an age differentiation here. That's not the issue." She sighed. "You brought this subject up because it was an important societal observation you made. Clearly, it bothers you. It goes against spiritual tenets and you feel the need to bring this behavior to people's attention. So?"

"I'm not humanity's mother and I'm not . . . ."

A deep growl disturbed the room's soft ambiance. Sally's eyes focused behind me.

I turned to Cheyenne. She growled again and began creeping forward.

In a flash, both Cheyenne and Rosie charged barking into the shadowy kitchen.

I looked at Sally and whispered, "We have a visitor."

"Oh my," she said, getting to her feet after I did. "Who?"

I shrugged while entering the now raucous kitchen. The only light was from a pewter rack of four burning votive candles I kept on the counter. By now, all the dogs were wildly barking up at the corner of the ceiling.

We stared at the spot.

"You see anyone?" Sally asked.

"Nope, but then that's not unusual, is it."

As if on cue, all the Yorkies trotted back into the living room as though nothing out of the ordinary had happened. Cheyenne gave a final growl and followed suit.

Sally looked about the room. We were alone looking up at an empty ceiling. "I feel like I've just been left holding the bag."

I laughed. "C'mon, there's nothing here now."

"Maybe the dogs heard a mouse scratching up in the wall."

I rolled my eyes. "Cheyenne's not an alarmist. She doesn't growl at mice, chipmunks, squirrels, birds, or big bugs. Nor is she a hunter. She's a guard dog. Her instincts are honed for intruders. She simply picked up on an unknown presence and began growling at it. Rosie, being the next sensitive one, caught it, too. Those two pointed it out to the others and all of them ended up with eyes glued to that ceiling."

"Maybe it wasn't the ceiling. Maybe it just sounded like it was coming from there, when it was actually coming from the floor upstairs."

I looked up. "Well? If that's the case, then it came from your bedroom closet. Why don't you go up and check it out."

"No, thanks," she quickly declined. Turning to leave the kitchen, she announced, "Dogs aren't barking anymore. It's gone now. Whatever it was is gone."

I followed her into the living room, picked up the dictionary and carted it back to my desk. Upon my return, I caught her eyeing the kitchen. "It left, Sally."

"For now," she responded.

"For now."

∞ ∞ ∞

"What were we talking about?"

"How terms are misused in a prejudicial manner. They're also used in a racist manner, too. Not racist in terms of demeaning necessarily, but racist in terms of maintaining separatism."

"How do you mean?"

"First of all, we're the people of earth–its populace. We're all God's children, God's earth children. We are humankind. That is who we are. We are all members of the human family. I can't stress that enough because it's the common gene that binds us all together, makes us all related to one another. The *primary* race of us all is the *human* race. And racism exists because people have lost sight of their primary heritage, their primary identity.

"Enter now the subclassification element of the *secondary* characteristics known as ethnicity. Herein lies the problem, for this is falsely perceived as the whole of one's identity. This, therefore, is where the focus is misplaced. The focus of personal identity is erroneously determined by *geographic* culture rather than the primary species of self, which is a human being.

"Identifying self by means of a specific geographic culture, such as African American, Asian, Hawaiian, Indian, Irish, Slavic, etc., begins to manifest the separatist ideology and shatters the unifying fact that we are, first and foremost, of the human race. It would be like trying to identify the 'who' of us by the clothing we wear instead of what's inside. Clothing is frivolous trapping as much as where we've traveled or what piece of land we were born on. So, the act of clinging to a specific geographic location and claiming that as an identity, diminishes one's beautiful totality and begins to break down species unity.

"The subject of genealogy exacerbates this; I mean, who cares if Geronimo was your great, great, great uncle? Who cares if you're related to Columbus or your family line can be traced to those who first came over on the Mayflower? Are you making *those* people *your* own identity? Anyway," I quipped, "people need to realize that they themselves could've been their own great, great grandma!

"Our spirits enter the physical as bodies being born into the human race of earth. These bodies are clothed in a wide variety of physical feature characteristics derived from the specific geographical culture of their parents. These physical 'clothing' characteristics are the ethnic traits. They are dressing only, not the 'who' of you. Racism, both aggressive and passive, is like separatism based on the kind of clothing one wears."

Sally had a question. "Passive racism?"

"That's when members of a specific ethnic culture actively perpetuate their separateness, their distinction from others."

"Passive racism is keeping one's *own* ethnic culture separate and aggressive racism is negativity or aggression toward *another*, different ethnic culture."

"Yes. In reality, both contribute to separatism. Separatism leads to ethnic arrogance. Ethnic arrogance leads to discrimination."

"I'd like to go back to something you said. I have a minor question."

"Sure."

"When you were giving examples of geographical cultures that people identified with, why did you say 'Indian' instead of 'native American?'"

"Do you mind if we get back to that later? It's a separate issue."

"All right."

The dogs had settled down. Pinecone was curled in my lap. Rosie and Punkin had wedged themselves on either side of me. Baby was with Sally and Cheyenne snoozed beside my chair. All was quiet.

My friend had concerns about what we were discussing.

"You're not saying that ethnic pride is wrong, are you?"

"Of course not. Ethnic diversity adds beautifully brilliant colors to the human race quilt. St. Patrick's Day parades, Cinco de Mayo fiesta celebrations, and such."

"What of the Million Man March?"

I didn't readily respond.

"Did you hear me?"

"I really don't want to go there. That was an example of racist and sexist passive separatism. That particular example is a completely different subject matter. That specific event carried an underlying agenda.

"Ethnic celebrations can be beautiful as long as they're kept in perspective, as long as people keep in mind that it's a secondary quality to their primary race designation as a human being. And that's the fly in the pie, isn't it. That's the crux of the whole issue—keeping perspective.

"Racism intensifies whenever one ethnic group claims an attitude of superiority over another. History bears this out time and time again. The lesson has not been grasped and learned. It hasn't sunk in. Caucasians have felt superiority over many different ethnic cultures. Palestinians against Israelis. Germans over Jews. Early Americans over the Indians and it goes on and on, ad nauseam. Instead of perceiving one another as human beings all related, people narrow their perspective down to an ethnic tunnel vision. Therefore, instead of recognizing each other as *relations*, people identify others as Hispanic, or White, or Asian . . . different. And 'different' means a non-relation."

"Native Americans . . . ." Sally began.

"That's a misnomer. I'll explain later."

She began again. "American Indians have a saying, 'All my relations,' that means all of life is related."

"It's a fact. It's a fact they have the saying and it's a fact that all life is indeed related."

My friend frowned. "Something's the matter."

"You and I both know what's the matter with that. AIM blacklists my writings and those of others like me on the sole basis of our ethnicity. I'm different from them; I'm not one of them, therefore I cannot write anything related to their culture. That's separatism. That's aggressive racism. That is not 'all my relations.'

"An Indian woman says she's going to organize a bookstore boycott of my writings because I have an Indian-sounding name when I'm not Indian . . . yet she has an Anglo-sounding name. That's ethnic arrogance. That's aggressive racism. That is not 'all my relations.'

"Among some cultural groups, I've watched a growing arrogance that's shifted them toward an attitude of ethnic isolation and superiority that's so aloof and dangerous that it's approaching personified deity—that all races save theirs is inferior.

"Our individual geographical culture can be celebrated as a beautiful heritage contributing to our overall uniqueness, but first and foremost, we are 'all relations in the human race.'"

Sally sighed. "Some people would think all that was deeply profound, yet it's reality in its most simplistic form." She hesitated before continuing. "Have you ever regretted that destiny presented your teacher as an ethnic individual?"

"Absolutely. With a great deal of contemplation given to hindsight, I feel the purpose of my mission could've been better served if she'd been a multicultural individual. Because her ethnicity was so strong, people completely lost sight of her *universal* spiritual knowledge and wisdom. Her teachings were never wholly ethnic ones, they encompassed the entire range of quantum spirituality." I smiled then. "That fact went way over AIM's head. All they zeroed in on was bloodline, nothing more meaningful than that. They never realized the vast scope and depth of my teacher's knowledge and that it encompassed the totality of universal physics and dipped heavily into the vast potentialities of cosmic consciousness.

"My teacher's ethnicity, in the end, served to narrow my message and compress it into a cultural one rather than one meant for all of humanity. It gave the inference of 'Indian'-specific beliefs rather than universal spiritual and quantum truths.

"Yes, I would've wished she'd chosen a neutral or mixed identity. Instead, it brought undue concerns and confusion because *quantum* (universal) spirituality has no ethnic parent, it is not possessed nor secreted away by any one culture. It is there for everyone. Quantum reality and its related spiritual aspects exist in and of themselves. They are held as a high sacred captive by no one and no one race.

"My move away from the Indian artwork for my book covers has been one of the few ways I could personally make the effort to present my message as a *pure* one that won't visually give the impression of being Indian-related in any way. Because of my mentor's ethnicity, people focused on her race rather than her important words. Readers made her Indian-ness an issue that overshadowed the profound wisdom she had to impart. That was wrong. I'm trying very hard to turn that around.

"Now," I said, "I want to address your former question that concerned my specific terminology in reference to the American Indian. If someone were born in Norway, they'd be a native Norwegian. If someone were born in Australia, they'd consider themselves to be 'native Australian.'"

Sally finished. "Someone born in America is a native American."

"There you are! Generally, the term 'native' applies to the region or *country* one is born in. The word 'native' is not an exclusive synonym for Indian. This concept is exemplified by someone born in India who identifies self as an East Indian or a native of India. All American Indians are native Americans (if they were, in fact, born here), but not all native Americans are American Indians. Furthermore, the American Indians can choose to give themselves a more definitive identity by calling themselves by their tribal association, such as Hopi Indian, Apache Indian, etc.

"In a way, it ties in with the issue of using proper terms for people and not mislabeling groups or concepts.

It relates to the importance of perspective, the use of prejudicial terminology and the practice of ethnic separatism. Factually speaking, you and I are each a native of America . . . native Americans because we were both born here and . . . ."

Cheyenne growled.

"Oh, Cheyenne, not again," I said. "Go back to sleep."

I reached my hand down to soothe her.

Sally glanced into the kitchen.

The Yorkies were sound asleep and I hoped they'd stay that way.

Cheyenne's second growl seemed half-hearted and I rubbed her ear. "Shhh, it's okay," I whispered. She released a heavy sigh and closed her eyes.

As the dogs gave in to the peacefulness of the room, an old memory passed through my mind and I clutched it before it vanished. While giving this thought some attention, I hadn't realized I'd been staring at my friend.

"Have I sprouted antennae?" she asked, jarring my mental focus. "What're you so intent on?"

"I was thinking about something a lady once said to me. She told me that I gave all my power away."

"And?"

"She was wrong."

"Of course she was wrong. Mary, when we were in the bookstore today I couldn't help but notice how the books on *power* have quadrupled. Has having power become such a high priority? It was ridiculous. There were how-to books on gaining personal power everywhere."

"Really. I hadn't noticed," I admitted.

"You didn't notice? The way to shamanic power, corporate power, sexual power, feminine power, the power makers, you name it and it was there."

"People are always looking for ways to get a handle on their lives," I said, "ways to be more in control."

"But," my friend frowned, "real power has nothing to do with control."

"No. No, it doesn't. At least not the control of others."

"Real power is love," she stated.

Our gaze met. "Real power is wisdom," I said.

She thought on that. "I disagree," came her counter.

"Why?"

"Because there's no greater force."

"I agree. Love is a force, an energy. Granted it's the most powerful one. Yet having power and having a powerful force is not the same thing. One can love a mate with a powerful force of energy and still not possess personal power. The capacity to love, even unconditional love, is on an entirely different level than personal power. Love is far greater than the power we're speaking about. Love is the breadth and depth of pure spirituality. It is of spirit, while power is transitory, fluid, and temporary when perceived by an overview perspective, and love is above all these. Love is above all. It's above all qualities associated with the attributes of human personality. Real personal power is not a force, but rather a subtle quality of beingness."

My friend mulled that over. "That's the crux of the issue then. Generally, personal power is perceived as being able to manipulate some type of control in one's life. Manipulation would be the key word with this. The power to manipulate situations and those around you; being the leader or the one who's recognized as possessing greater knowledge or qualities of leadership."

"Yes, and that's not real personal power. Real power cannot be sought after because it naturally settles within one's beingness of its own accord. It's a process of development. It could be compared to the efforts one continually puts forth by doing rain dances trying to force nature to comply with his or her own will, rather than accepting life until it rains and *then* standing out in it while it gently washes over one's beingness. One gains power in a *natural* manner through experiential living and learning, growing, ever-expanding evolution of the self by way of these life events. This evolutionary growth is called wisdom.

"Wisdom," I expanded, "has nothing to do with the level of one's attained knowledge or I.Q. rating. I've observed more wisdom from a sweet adolescent with Down's Syndrome than from a high-minded scholar. Schooling can't teach wisdom, nor can it instill the power it carries. Age isn't a factor in regard to wisdom, either. I've crossed paths with more than a couple exceptionally wise young adults and their inner power radiated through their auras like the gentle waves on a tranquil sea."

I extended my arm over the side of the chair and ran my hand over the length of Cheyenne's fluffy back. Gently stroking her fur, I continued. "We know that personal power is wisdom. We know what wisdom isn't. It's not intelligence, age or attained knowledge. So, what is wisdom?"

Sally's eyes twinkled in the dancing firelight. "Having street smarts."

I liked her response and expressed my amusement of it. "I like that! I like it a lot. It was a bottom-line answer because wisdom is having the tools to survive life. Being street-wise is being life-wise; having the wisdom it takes to travel through life and experience it in a noble and stress-reduced manner. That's *power.*

"So, that brings us to the next question . . . the nitty-gritty. What are the tools of wisdom? What qualities define wisdom?"

"I think *acceptance* is a safe answer," she replied. "Acceptance reeks of wisdom. Acceptance carries incredible power. It precludes judgment. Acceptance is the terminator of untold negative emotions that can destroy one's relationships, health, life, and even self."

"Life is the same as self."

"No, I meant 'life' as representing one's personal circle of conditional living factors, such as job, marital status, friends, social arena, etc.—their lifestyle. I meant 'self' to represent the physical self and the destruction of same through emotional and psychological self-mutilation or, ultimately, suicide."

My clarification was acknowledged and I continued. "Acceptance is wisdom. Wisdom is power. Therefore, *acceptance is power*. Some folks view acceptance as being a wimp. It's not. Neither is it lying down and playing dead or letting others walk all over you. It's not being any kind of a weakling. It's the strength and power of a thorough understanding of behavioral diversity among humanity.

"With wisdom of acceptance one has the power to easily override negative emotions, reactions, and attitudes. It instills the power to gracefully accept the bad behavior of others without inciting negativity within self. This is not apathy. This is the power of wisdom.

"Acceptance is an absolute. It possesses the quality of nonjudgment. Its world view is not fragmented into nations or races, but rather sees everyone as a human being. This then means that racism, sexism, and prejudice do not exist within the heart and mind of one who has attained this powerful tool of wisdom.

"Living through each day, week, and year of one's life is to experience a thrilling and unending presentation of gifts. Some gifts aren't needed and, truth be told, can actually be unwanted, yet they are 'accepted' with grace just the same. Life's misfortunes are presented along with life's blessings, both received with a great depth of understanding when one has the power of acceptance."

My friend voiced a thought. "Understanding. You said 'understanding.' That's a key quality of acceptance, isn't it."

"Absolutely. It's the understanding that keeps acceptance from being the quality of an automaton. Acceptance doesn't mean that we go through life like robots that have no responses, no reactive thoughts or actions. It's the 'understanding' element that impels us to make alternate choices and plans when life presents misfortunes or paths that somehow go awry.

"I'm not saying one necessarily has to understand the precise *reasons* for misfortune, but rather that one understands that misfortunes are a natural aspect of life. Realizing the natural reality of the good with the bad. The knowing that life is fluid and the wiseness of floating on the current whichever way it meanders; understanding the futility of fighting against the natural current of life. That's the understanding we're talking about."

Sally reminded me of a time I spent spinning my mind into a tangle of spiraling circles trying to find reason and rationale for some people's behavior. She pointed out that my healing accelerated only after I let it go with acceptance and the realization that trying to find reasons wasn't important—that it was only holding me back.

"Yes," I freshly recalled. "Acceptance is also letting go. It's releasing the compelling urge to understand another's behavior. Acceptance is the impetus that soothingly eases one forward into a gentle state where healing begins to take hold. Acceptance brings a growing measure of inner serenity."

∞ ∞ ∞

Being reminded of my experience with some people's irrational behavior and my unfruitful attempts to understand them emphasized another associated element of the situation.

"Having acceptance doesn't mean one lives in an emotional vacuum. Accepting the behavior of others doesn't mean your emotional responses are deadened; you can still be hurt, disappointed, or saddened. Yet having that acceptance is the singular quality that eases the personal harm that was inflicted." I smiled. "For me, it was like a winch that pulled me up out of the mental mire I'd gotten myself into while trying to understand someone's behavior."

"A winch. That's a good analogy," Sally replied with a bright smile of her own. "Acceptance not only keeps one on solid ground, it has the capability of hauling one back onto solid footing. I watched that happen with you. It works."

The aspen log recently placed in the woodstove softly burned with quiet amber flames.

All the furry little people were twitching with sweet dreams.

Reflections waltzed over the wood walls while wisps of fragrant cedar filled the senses.

For several tranquil moments we were silent. Voicing past experiences and making references to them usually inspired a period of reminiscing; each of us remembering our own part of the event.

Knowing that certain memories were unproductive to review, I was first to break our reverie. "Acceptance isn't the only quality of wisdom," I said.

Prepared to return to the moment, my friend immediately responded to my statement. "*Patience* is power. Patience is a quality of wisdom."

"That's right, yet patience has a twin. Patience holds hands with *perseverance*. Waiting. The waiting for something to happen can literally destroy one. Impatience causes stress and stress wears down the immune system quicker than any other life factor. Impatience keeps one focused on a singular element, which, in turn, prevents an awareness of the living moment. Impatience breeds negativity. It makes one crabby and short with others. It can steal life away. Impatience and the anxiety it creates can become a cancer that eats away everything in one's life, even the physical self."

"You're talking long-term impatience, right?"

"Right."

"Because short-term waiting can intensify a response to an outcome or event."

"You mean like an expectant father pacing in the delivery waiting room?"

She nodded. "Yes, but I was specifically referring to our waiting to see if everything fell into place to get this cabin."

That brought a wide smile to my face. "That was anticipation! Sure, when an outcome is imminent, the element of anticipation accompanies the waiting period and that aspect serves to intensify the manifested event. Short-term waiting can sweeten the pot. It's the long-term waiting that is destructive by stealing away the present.

"Patience and perseverance give the power to have goals without allowing those same goals to overshadow and darken daily living. Goals are of the future and, having the wisdom to realize that perspective gives one power to live every day to the fullest with patience, while holding on to those goals with perseverance. With these strong qualities of wisdom, you give yourself the power to accomplish both. And, I'm pleased to add, this prevents inner tension and turmoil, bringing a good measure of serenity to one's life."

Sally's head slowly went from side to side. "Almost everyone I know is waiting for something. Some of them are in a constant state of irritability, while some are continually depressed, and a few have a nice 'whatever' attitude. The difference between their personalities and demeanor is remarkable."

"Oh, yes. It's noticeable, isn't it. And something you just said summed up what power and wisdom is."

My friend's brow creased. "Something I just said?"

I nodded with an amused expression.

She mentally reviewed her words. Stumped, she said, "What? What'd I say?"

"You compressed the meaning of power and wisdom into a nutshell . . . a single-word nutshell."

Thinking.

Smiling with anticipation.

"I give," she sighed.

"Attitude! Having the right *attitude* is wisdom. It's *power*!"

An inaudible growl reverberated along Cheyenne's back and through my fingers resting there. Before I could soothe her, she and Rosie raced barking into the office. The other dogs followed suit, with Sally and me on their tails. All of them were ferociously barking up at the skylights above my desk.

I turned and sped up the stairs to race through Sally's room. Peering through her dormer window, I looked down on the skylights below. I saw nothing out of the ordinary, not even a bat or other night critter that could've found its way to the roof.

"See anything?" Sally called.

"Nope. Not a thing," I said, descending the stairs.

"What do you think they're barking at?"

I shrugged with the oddity and we both headed toward the front door with the same thought in mind—outside we'd have a better view.

Once on the covered porch, we walked the length several times, then quickly made our way down the steps. Checking beneath the porch revealed nothing unusual.

We scanned the night sky.

Nothing.

The house became suddenly silent.

The dogs had stopped barking.

The two of us stood out in the moonlight. Though the silvery valley was ethereally beautiful to gaze upon, our eyes were automatically drawn to the twinkling vastness above.

Shooting stars.

A slowly arcing satellite.

Sparkling planets.

All was as it should be.

We returned to the house, where the little ones greeted us with whimpers and wagging tails. Now that we were back inside, everything was right in their world. Within minutes they were back in the living room, settling down as if no disturbance had occurred.

After getting myself a glass of ice water, I, too, returned to the room and sat on the hearth before the fire. Sally was already in her place on the love seat. She was placing her gun in the drawer of the end table.

"I didn't notice you'd had your gun," I commented.

"You think we'd go outside to investigate a disturbance without it? I grabbed it when you were upstairs. Have any feelings as to what got the dogs riled?"

"We didn't find anything outside, but it had that altered feel to it, didn't it."

She'd noticed it, too. "I hate it when it feels like that. It's so still. Nothing moving. No sounds. There's always night sounds out there."

"Except when it feels altered."

"Did you feel the Starborn around?"

"Funny you should ask," I said, shaking my head in response. "More like the residual effect of their presence . . . after they've left."

My friend lit an incense stick. "What's going on? Sometimes when I'm working late down here on the book illustrations after you've gone to bed, I feel like I'm not alone. It's a very creepy sensation. And . . . and twice last week, when you were bedridden for those two days with your wrenched back, I checked on you during the night and there was some sort of light on you."

Surprise lit my face. "You never mentioned that before. A light? Maybe it was a moonlight reflection on the paneled wall."

She shot me a disgusted look. "I know a reflection when I see one. Jeez, Mary, I'm not a dunce. Give me some credit."

"I'm sorry. I just always try to find a physical reason for things that appear unexplainable. So . . . what sort of light was this?"

"Well, it surprised me so much, my first thought was that it was something that wasn't meant for me to share or know about. You were sound asleep and it felt like this was some type of intimate happening between it and you."

I frowned with that. "Intimate?"

A wry smile tipped the corner of her mouth. "That wasn't the right word. It felt serene, like a companionable presence."

"I understand what you mean, but what *kind* of light was it? What were its characteristics? Was it a twinkling pinpoint like the ones I've seen out in the woods? Was it like a flame or ray?"

"No, no. It was a diffused glow that was encompassing you from your head to your hips. No specific outline to speak of other than a large circular glow that nearly lit up the entire room."

"Mmmm. And the dogs, the dogs on the bed weren't aware of it?"

"You were all sound asleep, even them."

"What were your feelings about this light? Your first impression?"

"God, Mary, there's so much that happens around here that I've stopped trying to identify what all the unexpected sights and sounds are. Instead, I focus on friend or foe?"

"Foe? No foes get near here."

She released a weighted sigh. "Well, yes," came the admission, "I know that, but there's no way I want a private run-in with those Starborn guys. That's your department and . . . ."

I laughed. "So, *they're* who you're referring to as 'foe'—someone you'd rather not come face-to-face with."

She sheepishly grinned. "Anyway, I didn't feel any negativity, more like I was intruding, so I went back to my room. I had the strong impression that the light could've been a presence that was comforting and protecting you. You were engulfed in it."

"When you went back to bed, did you pull the covers up over your head?" I teased.

"You're making fun of me."

"Nah, you know better than that. I was just kidding. So . . . this happened both nights?"

She nodded. "Those were the only nights I checked on you. Who knows how often it happens."

"It couldn't have been my aura you were seeing?"

"Will you stop with that! It wasn't in the shape of a human outline. You were completely within it, as if it were emanating *from* you, your heart area."

"Okay. All right, let's let it go, because I've no idea what it was," I said, returning to my chair after tossing a small aspen log on the fire.

"Aren't you even curious?" she asked.

I shrugged. "It was obviously a peaceful and loving presence, if it was a presence. I don't need to know more. You want to go back to our conversation on power or did you have some other subject in mind?"

"If the dogs will stop charging around the house at shadows, yes, I'd like to continue on power."

"Okay. We were talking about power being right attitude. That's really what it comes down to. Most all of wisdom's qualities are some type of attitude or perspective. Now, one of these is probably a quality you'd never think to associate with wisdom and that's *silence*."

"Mmmm," she mused. "Interesting. I wouldn't have thought of that, but it makes perfect sense. Knowing when to hold your tongue is wise. You yourself have said that silence is power. What's left unsaid can make a huge impact sometimes. There are situations when one's silence speaks louder than words."

"Silence goes along with acceptance. When you have acceptance of people's behavior, you naturally withhold certain responsive comments or opinions. Your knee-jerk reactions aren't made evident. Of course, this doesn't mean that you don't internally experience these reactions, you just don't voice them aloud to others. Reserving comments and opinions is also a preventative form of wisdom, in that it prevents one from being accused of trying to control another's life through continual advice or opinionated viewpoints.

And silence in regard to one's own life problems prevents an individual from being perceived as a whiner or one who is constantly seeking sympathy."

My friend wasn't convinced she agreed with this last point. "Silence can also conceal personal, painful experiences that *should* be exposed. There are times when it's not productive to keep certain life events to yourself because this can leave one open to slander or misrepresented scenarios down the line. If nobody but you is aware of what you've been enduring, it's too easy for another individual to speak out by broadcasting altered details and fabricated stories."

My eyes locked hard on hers. "I wish you'd stop bringing up the past, but, since you have, we'll look at it. You're talking about the need to defend oneself against falsehoods. You're talking about sharing heartache, so others will be apprised of an ongoing situation in one's life, therefore, down the road, another person can't turn the situation around on you. You're talking about covering one's butt with witnesses."

"Something like that," she replied.

"Well, I'll admit that I've wondered if I should've done that. It would've most likely prevented some additional heartache and humiliation I experienced toward the end. Yet I've always viewed that type of sharing with others as placing a worrisome burden on family, friends, and associates. Everyone has personal life situations or relationships they have to deal with. Why burden them with mine, too? I've always thought that way, so I've always dealt privately with heart pain. My pain shouldn't be another's."

She still didn't agree. "If someone always bears their burdens, pains, and heartaches in silence, nobody knows how they feel; no one else is aware of what that individual has been going through or is dealing with."

"So? It's not nice to burden others. I'm not a crybaby."

She released a deep sigh. "God, you can be difficult sometimes," she spouted.

"I'm not trying to be difficult. Silence is wisdom. Silence is strength. And I'm still here, aren't I?"

"Yes, but look at the added pain your silence cost you!"

"Cost? What did it cost me? Some extra heartache. Some humiliation from false assumptions and ignorant gossip caused by someone's vindictive innuendos spoken to defend the actions of self. Sally, that sort of behavior is so shallow and . . . ."

"Not shallow enough to make you immune to its effects," she countered.

"I'm still here. I'm the same person I always was. I will continue being that same person, living my life as I always have and, know what?"

"Enlighten me."

"I will continue in silence. Now, more than ever, I'm convinced of the wiseness of remaining private. Showing my heart doesn't work, at least with things of a personal nature. I've seen the proof of that. I'm not a complainer, never have been, and I'm not about to start being one at this late date. Just because one situation may have personally worked out better for me if I'd shared ongoing events with others doesn't mean I need to change my ways. Silence has always served me well."

"Yes, it has, but the planted innuendos live on."

"So be it."

"You're not concerned?"

"Should I be?"

Clearly, she didn't understand my response. "Rumors that you've changed could harm your work."

I didn't reply.

"Mary?"

Silence.

Waiting.

When I did respond it was with a soft whisper. "Jesus, too, loved everyone."

"What'd you say?"

"Jesus, too, loved everyone. Everywhere he journeyed he loved everyone. So little is written about his great love of life. I may bring that to light one day.

"Anyway, he had such a high exuberance for participating in life's joys and entertainments. He looked forward to being invited to partake in the banquets of various festivities and sharing a wide variety of dishes people offered him at their family table. He laughed and he danced. And he loved everyone. Wild rumors spread far and wide about his activities and behavior. Jealousy, prejudice, vindictiveness, whatever negative attitude, spawned rumors born of personal insecurity. Yet . . . what qualities of Jesus survived history?"

"Point taken," she conceded.

"Let's get back to the power of silence's wisdom. Silence is wise when it circumvents inflicting emotional pain on others. There're limitless ways this can be utilized throughout life. Many expressed opinions, without intentionally meaning to be, can be cruel and hurtful to another. This type of silence refers to guarding one's speech. It's always wise to guard one's responses in a conversation. Oftentimes people's feelings can be hurt by thoughtlessness or a seemingly innocent comment. Silence can be a gentle expression of kindness. It can be utilized to avert arguments and discord. It can be a peacemaker.

"Have you noticed how much people talk?" I unexpectedly asked, without waiting for an answer. "Everywhere you go there's endless chatter surrounding you. In restaurants, on the street, players and employees in the casino, while shopping, in the workplace; there's a constant din of yakking assaulting one's senses. Most of it is trite, petty, or gossip, complaints, or grumbles. Yakkity-yak."

That appeared to amuse my friend. "All that yakkity-yak emphasizes the fact that talk is cheap."

"Why?"

"Why what?"

"Talk doesn't have to be cheap, so . . . why is it?" I pushed.

"Because people don't realize that silence is golden, that silence is wisdom. They'd much rather be titillated by juicy gossip or give out random advice to others or be tearful crybabies and play a 'woe is me' game. A lot of talk is done to get attention or sympathy or make a bid for some type of control."

"Why?"

"Why? Because their focus on self demands it. Their egos call out to be noticed and stroked."

That answer was a direct hit. "Why?" I prompted further.

My question surprised her. She thought about it a bit. She grinned wide. "They're giving away their power! They're throwing away the power of silence. They're exposing their lack of wisdom."

"Yes! *That's* how one's personal power is given away . . . thrown away . . . given up. Real power, when it's a way of life, can never be given away. Only through nonuse is it laid fallow and wasted."

"So, this lady who said you were giving away all your power had no understanding of what power is. She thought it was knowledge and energy."

"Right. Real power, when regularly exercised, revitalizes itself. The continual utilization of real power serves to strengthen it. Think of real power as being your muscles. The more you use them, through routine exercise, the stronger they become. Their strength isn't 'given away' through depletion by using them.

"Take acceptance, for example. One may have to initially train herself to accept this or that in the beginning, but after a time, it becomes easier and easier to do until it's an automatic responsive attitude. It gains increased strength through utilization."

"It becomes a conditioned response," Sally concluded.

"Yes. It becomes a wise response that increases the level of power in one's life."

Sally's mental gears were smoking.

"What now?" I inquired.

"Having several of these wisdom qualities can frequently give the wrong impression to others."

"I can think of several responses to that statement. I'll begin by asking you how so?"

"Having acceptance can appear as unemotionalism, insensitivity. Patience and perseverance can be interpreted as possessing . . . well . . . being a dreamer or holding onto an obsessive idea."

I smiled. "Pie in the sky?"

"Sort of."

"What else?"

"Silence can be perceived as ignorance or a type of apathy."

"But you and I know that isn't so. These types of 'perceptions' are individualized interpretations and personal opinions. They are *assumptions*. And one of my other thoughts that came with your initial statement had to do with what these 'impressions' relate to."

My friend frowned as though I didn't understand the precise issue. "They relate to misinterpretation of power and how that misinterpretation makes you look."

"*Who* 'look'?" I questioned with purpose.

"*You* look!" Her hands immediately flew up in the air with her realized epiphany. "Oh God! I get it! The 'you' is an egocentric issue! To care what people assume about you is to focus on the 'I' of self! And that's a completely separate concept from power."

I smiled. "Did you think I was ignorant of what people secretly thought of me when I didn't join in a conversation that I believed to be trite, gossipy, or metaphysically irrelevant or ridiculous? Don't you think I'm fully aware of their speechless, mental confoundment when I reply to a silly question with an equally silly response and then watch how the acknowledgment of my intended humor totally escapes them? Goes over their heads?

"Sally, why should I care if I don't participate in a frivolous conversation and people think it's because I'm not knowledgeable on the subject? If people want to yak about and go into awe-filled states over every corny book they believe was written by Starborn, let them; I'm not going to waste my time discussing invalid issues. That's only one example.

"My point is that the 'I' of me doesn't care a whit about wild or false 'impressions' or assumptions. That's why those old rumors didn't keep bothering me. I'm more comfortable with my silence. The ego aspect of what folks assume from that silence never affects me. That attitude is not one that I one day suddenly decided to have, either. That attitude comes hand-in-hand with understanding and utilizing silence. That attitude is power all by itself."

Sally voiced an observation. "By the example you gave, people assume that someone's silence, their reticence to discuss something, may evidence ignorance, while their own discourse proves knowledge when, in actuality, the reverse is more often true. Silence shows wisdom. Yakking exposes ignorance."

"Not always," I reminded.

"Well, no, not always. Just much of the time," she corrected.

∞ ∞ ∞

Pinecone jumped into my lap and curled into a ball so small and tight that it still amazed me to realize she was a real dog. She was like a miniature toy, no bigger than some of the dogs' stuffed playthings in the toy box. With my fingertips I gently stroked her silky head.

"Silence is wisdom in one other way," I said. "Refraining from giving people answers to certain questions is wise. This lack of response is wise when they won't, for one reason or another, take personal responsibility for their life; when they refuse to make their own decisions.

"Frequently, people need to go through their own reasoning process that brings them to a conclusion or decision. This reasoning process is vitally important because it clarifies muddy issues and brings a greater, fuller understanding. It clears away the fog, so to speak. Giving out answers to another's life questions steals away that individual's power to work through problems. It steals away their power to reason things out and derive concluding theories on their own. It steals away their beautiful gift of free will. It reeks of control. And that brings us to another quality of the power of wisdom."

"Control," Sally said.

"Yes, but more specifically, *responsibility*. Personal responsibility. A minute ago I was talking about advice people seek and the searching for answers to their questions. I need to specify that these advisements, answers, and questions only refer to the kind directly associated with their personal life. I'm not referring to talking to a professional such as a physician or psychiatrist or seeking advice on how to fix a plumbing leak. I'm not referring to asking around for recommendations regarding a reliable roofer. I'm talking about situations in one's personal life in regard to behavioral choices and decision making. This distinction needs to be clear. So the point of this is friends, family, and associates. These naturally include psychics.

"By asking advice from any of those people, folks are admitting that they don't have control of their lives, can't make a decision, don't want the responsibility of a decision, and want someone else to tell them what to do. This gives power to others to control their lives. They let themselves become manipulated. They offer others power over them on a polished, silver platter.

"Now remember, this is adult-to-adult. I'm not talking about a child seeking advice from a parent, because that's entirely different. That's natural. Nobody walks in another's shoes. No one can live another's life. Everyone is unique. Everyone, an individual. Unique paths, goals, personalities, talents, education, etc. And since nobody is anyone's clone—yet—nobody can say what's best for another because they haven't lived the same life, experienced the same events, felt the identical emotional responses, or thought the same thoughts. It's wise to realize that your life is yours alone. Only you end up answering for how your life was enacted. It's having power when one understands that the absolute administration of that life is under nobody's control but your own. It's your domain to rule . . . no one else's. That realization is power. It's wisdom. Taking the *responsibility* for the handling and utilization of that knowledge is power to the nth degree. Personal power is being in total control of one's own life."

Sally's brow creased. "Every time someone goes to a psychic means they're weak? Well," she immediately rephrased, "not necessarily 'weak,' but shirking their responsibility? Fearful of making their own decisions."

"Yes, that's exactly what it says . . . unless, of course, they're just going for the heck of it . . . for the entertainment value and aren't serious. It's when they're serious that they're admitting to the world that they want to be 'told' how to proceed or which way to go. It says they can't live in the moment and crave a knowing of the future. It screams of ignorance of the real power they have. It says they want someone else to control their lives, someone else to direct their footfalls through life. Laziness and fear of making mistakes lead folks to psychics. These people give up their own power because of these fears and cravings for quick answers."

Sally concluded that psychics would be out of business if people realized their own powerful potential that personal responsibility opens up for them. "They see psychics as having the power when, in reality, it's the same power the seekers are denying self of."

"I like how you worded that. That's interesting and it's a powerful statement in and of itself. No one can control your life unless you let them. Everyone has to take personal responsibility for that control. Nothing prevents one from putting their own foot down in order to regain that control and responsibility, especially if there's any shred of doubt about the outside advice received. Following your *own* mind and inner promptings is power! That's wisdom! Otherwise, one allows others to lead them through life. Otherwise, you give away your power by giving others power over you."

"So you're saying that when people go to a psychic they don't understand the meaning of power, that they think it's some ultrasecret knowledge the psychic has."

"We've already established that real power is not knowledge. Yes, those who seek out psychics think the psychic's alleged *skill*, their assumed *knowing*, is the power."

"And you're saying that these seekers don't realize that real power is *personal control* of their lives and that they give that over to the psychic."

"Yes. That's what I'm saying. And now you're going to tell me that what I've just said would turn all the psychics against me." I smiled. "Probably only those who charge people for the control they've been handed."

"You're speaking against new age thought."

"I'm not a new ager. I'm not a new age writer. I write *spiritual philosophy!* I can't help any category cubbyhole I've been shoved in. People have come to know me as a free thinker—telling how it is by way of cutting through the crap and giving the essential bottom line. They crave power and I tell them what real power is and also what it's not. I've no interest in shading the truth with colors that people prefer to gaze on or have a desire to see. White is white . . . not gray. If someone comes to me and asks the same sorts of questions they ask a psychic, what do you think I'd tell them?"

Sally grinned. "I'd rather not say."

Her response brought a smile to my face. "Rudeness doesn't count. Neither do four-letter words. I'd give them back their own power instead of taking it from them. I'd tell them I'd offer up prayers for their success in finding their own answers.

"Self-discovery is a beautiful event. Knowing one is in full control of one's life is a powerful feeling, not for the sake of having 'control' per se, but for the *freedom* it instills. The freedom to make choices and decisions without your perspective being colored or slanted by the opinions of others. The freedom from dependence on others as one gains self-confidence. Knowing one's mind. Reliance on self. Trusting self. These qualities come with taking personal responsibility. They are real power.

"Responsibility leads to the wisdom quality of *individuality* and the free expression of same. I think it's a given that every person on this planet is unique unto him or herself. Everyone is a beautifully unique individual. To have no fear or reservations about expressing that individuality is to have real power.

"This intertwines with acceptance. Realizing one's uniqueness and expressing it openly shows you accept the fact that you don't have to conform to any mores or generally accepted guidelines that may constrict the real you. It means you don't allow yourself to be affected by prejudice or other types of negative or ignorant attitudes. You wisely accept the behavior of others without allowing it to alter self in any way. You're confident in your beliefs and philosophy. You have the freedom to dress however you choose without any sense of feeling out of place. You're not hesitant to pursue unpopular issues for fear of ridicule. One who expresses self is never anyone's puppet and can rarely be manipulated. This freedom of expressing one's uniqueness is far from self-love, but is rather closely associated with recognizing one's inner beingness . . . the real 'who' of you. When you're true to that beingness, you're not fearful of recrimination just because you disagree on an issue or do things differently or blaze a new path. Being yourself is wonderfully liberating. Being yourself is power. It's wisdom. Having the power to freely express your beingness brings the wisdom of understanding that all people are as diverse in their individuality as the birds of the air, the fish in the sea and, in that understanding, do we celebrate all of life."

Sally added a comment. "Real power has quite a few qualities. I suppose there's more you want to add."

I nodded. "Care to guess?"

"Gentleness. An *inner serenity* is power. Wouldn't that automatically come along with acceptance?"

"Yes, after acceptance comes a natural, ingrained response; when it's an *instinctual* reaction. You see, sometimes people think they have acceptance, but they use it selectively." I shook my head. "Nuh-uh, that doesn't work. Using it that way isn't integrating it into one's true behavioral pattern. Using it in a selective manner isn't wisdom . . . nor is it power. Selective use of any one of wisdom's qualities never instills gentleness and inner serenity, because that behavior isn't true, isn't part of one's honest beingness. When it is true, serenity abides within.

"Again, I have to stress that having gentleness and serenity does not mean one is a doormat. And it doesn't mean you're emotionless either. It means you know the wisdom of controlling emotions and having the power to do so. This serenity is a unique state of being. While living among the various vulgarities of society, it's like carrying around a peaceful garden within your beingness and sitting on a sun-warmed bench in the tranquil center of it. This is not fantasy, nor is it a form of escapism. It's real. It's powerful."

My friend expressed some thoughts on this. "Serenity would automatically keep one from jumping to conclusions, because the individual would have the inner calm to analyze a situation and reason it out."

"Sure. Irrationality and impetuosity aren't evidenced in such a personality."

"Also," she added, while Baby rearranged herself in Sally's lap, "this personal serenity would have a soothing influence on others, wouldn't it? Since this calm would radiate from one's aura, it seems to me that others would benefit from it in some way."

My gaze was drawn to the changing firelight reflections on the gleaming wood walls. "Serenity's warmth and tranquillity radiate out from one and reflects upon the beingness of others like this firelight is giving a warm luster to that wall. Though this physical light doesn't penetrate deeper than the wall's surface, serenity does penetrate into the beingness of others." I smiled. "Though sometimes," I cautioned, "Serenity can make others sleepy. Being around this type of individual can bring on waves of calm and deep tranquillity, almost like having taken a mild sedative."

And with that, our dialogue paused while we took a few golden moments to enjoy the room's sweet peacefulness.

The fire softly burned.

The clock's pendulum voiced the cabin's steady heartbeat.

Dream whimpers from the little furry people brought feelings of a warm fullness of heart through their companionship and love for us.

These soft evenings were a blessing I counted. My life was full.

∞ ∞ ∞

I rose from the chair and carried Pinecone with me over to the breakfront, where I lit another cedar stick. "Of all the scents we've tried," I said, "this High Mountain Cedar is my favorite; it's me. I love it when we return home from a day away and I catch the cedar scent after walking inside. It's so homey to me."

"It is nice," Sally agreed. "It's a woodsy, mountain fragrance. It fits you."

I returned to my chair.

Pinecone closed her eyes again.

"There're a couple more qualities of wisdom's power left to talk about. Want to finish the subject?" I asked.

"We've come this far. Might as well carry it through."

"Understanding *value*. This is closely associated with having priorities lined up right. Understanding value has nothing to do with money or finances. The type of value that's related to wisdom isn't connected to anything of a touchable nature. We're not talking real estate or mutual funds here. We're talking about the *spiritual* value of good deeds, words, and thoughts. These contain great power. I mean, really powerful energies. Potential enough to move mountains!"

A challenging look that said, "check your credibility" came from across the room. "Was that a gross exaggeration or what you writers call poetic license?"

"Well," I sheepishly corrected, "maybe not mountains . . . maybe hills."

She grinned without further comment.

I couldn't resist voicing a playful jab back. "You're going to make sure I stay on the straight and narrow, aren't you."

"You do have a tendency to get carried away at times."

"And you don't?"

"I'm not the messenger."

"That ends that round, doesn't it," I concluded. "Anyway, my 'poetic license' was meant to characterize the incredible energy capabilities of *unconditional goodness*. We hear so much of unconditional love and never anything of unconditional goodness."

"I've never heard the term before," Sally said. "Is this something new from you?"

I didn't immediately reply because I didn't know. I'd never heard the term either. "It just came out my mouth," I grinned. "I think the Crone in me said it. Anyway, it would be similar to the 'random acts of kindness' notion, but much more powerful—leaving out the 'random' and replacing it with *continual* or maybe *living*. Continual unconditional goodness would be the idea. Not random or once in a while, but a *living* way of life.

"Wisdom is understanding the value of these practices and the power they carry. This kind of way of life is being a spiritual activist. Acting on every opportunity to spread goodness in one's life not only has the power to uplift people and overall vibrations, it comes back around to self by way of the immediate benefit of personal fulfillment. This fulfillment isn't a goody-two-shoes kind of thing, either. It's a natural spiritual warmth that fills one's total beingness following an act of goodness. The value of such behavior and its return benefits are immeasurable.

"Sometimes the exercising of this power can present interesting realizations. Whenever I give away something of mine that people perceive has monetary value, the recipient never fails to be reluctant to take it because of its *monetary* aspect, while I see it as the *giving* having the real value. Yet the act of receiving has value, too. Appreciation has spiritual value in that it's a blessing few realize." I paused for a moment to lock eyes with my friend's. "I notice that you practice unconditional goodness all the time."

She frowned. "Me? When?"

That amused me. "See? You do it so automatically that you don't even realize you're doing it."

Evidently she thought I was pulling her leg. "Give me an example," she challenged.

"Okay. Last winter, when Steve and his friend delivered our wood, you invited them inside to warm up. You not only sent them on their way with drinks to take along, you also gave them our two new pairs of leather work gloves."

"Well . . . they didn't have gloves and it was cold!"

"See what I mean? You giving those new gloves away put me to shame because, when I saw you hand them over, my first thought was 'what is she doing? We just bought those!' then I caught myself and felt good about what you'd done. You do that a lot, you know."

"Do what?"

"Give our things away. If you hear that somebody needs something and we have it . . . it's theirs. Gone. Out the door."

"That upsets you," she responded with growing concern.

I laughed. "Nope. Think it's funny! It amuses the hell out of me. Sally, that's what unconditional goodness is all about. Especially when it's done so naturally that it's instinctive.

"You want more examples?" I asked without expecting an answer. "What about the time you noticed the elderly lady trying to push her full cart of groceries through the rain and you spun the car around, loaded her and her sacks in the car and drove her home?

What about giving hitchhiking casino workers rides to work, even when you're headed home and have to turn around and go out of your way back to town? Or the time you stopped to help those ladies in the Cadillac get unstuck from the snowdrift they slid in?"

"I got stuck, too," she recalled.

"That's not the point. And you gave someone your shirt that they'd expressed admiration for. You give needy people money and . . . ."

"You do too!" she snapped back. "All right, you've convinced me. Let's move on."

"You don't like it when your good points are focused on, do you."

"It's embarrassing."

"Why?"

"Because it's just part of who I am, and things I do like that shouldn't be seen as anything special."

I grinned. "Exactly. Let's move on." I purposely hesitated then. "Well? I could still give you more examples of you . . . ."

"Mary!"

"Just kidding. We're moving on now. We were talking about spiritual value before we got sidetracked by unconditional goodness. The twin quality of value is *priority*. Understanding value begets a natural sequential order of correct priorities in one's life. What does that mean? One example would be the perspective of 'Living the Moment,' staying in the Now in spite of strong goals and dreams for the future, in spite of one's *wants*.

"By making the Now the number-one priority, life is lived to the fullest and is loaded with rich experiences that would otherwise go unnoticed and, consequently, unappreciated. Living for tomorrow places one's consciousness on the future instead of the moment.

Living for tomorrow is not *living* because this mental focus causes deep anxiety that, of itself, is a personality-altering emotion. In turn, this brings about stressed relationships and a warped perspective of the present. A preoccupation with tomorrow impedes an appreciation for the moment."

"Having dreams, plans, and life goals gives added purpose to life," Sally added. "These represent accomplishments to attain and work toward. They provide direction, yet without maintaining a prioritized perspective of these, I've seen lives ruined over them. They become an obsession, an all-consuming passion that overtakes a life with stress and anxiety."

"What's worse," I said, "is when the plans and goals don't manifest or they don't manifest according to one's long-held blueprint, thereby causing heartbreak or depression, resulting in false feelings of personal failure. That wouldn't happen if goals were not framed in the rigidness of a specifically detailed mental picture. Life is too fluid for that. Its current is an ever-changing flow and cannot be forced uphill or through natural barriers. This realization is wise to remember. 'Going with the flow' is not an idle cliché, it's wisdom. Keeping this little bit of wisdom in mind gives one the power to accept the unexpected in life and to float around the barriers with ease and continue on—forward—instead of being caught up against the barrier by fighting its very existence. Life is ever-changing. Life is fluid. We must be, too.

"Materialistically speaking, having the right priorities shows wisdom." I laughed then. "Having indoor plumbing holds more value to me than winning the Colorado lottery."

A wry smile came back at me. "That's because you've gone for days without water when the generator went out and we had to leave it at the shop for an overhaul."

"You've got a point. Yet, even before that, when I spent some time contemplating the value of things, I concluded that it was the basics–the necessities of life–that made me content. Having hygiene facilities, enough food to subsist on, a clean bed, and a roof over my head were more than many people on this planet had and I counted them as blessings. This realization lessened the perceived value of all other material goods and I began giving possessions away. Money was viewed in a totally different light, too. As long as I have enough to make the basic monthly living expenses, anything above that is a blessing I can share with others."

I wanted to finish up the subject of personal power. "The last quality of wisdom's power is *respect.*"

"All my relations," she interjected.

"Yes. Having a true and deep respect for all of life. Many people claim to have this respect, yet few do because it means no prejudicial attitudes: no sexism, no racial, religious, or ethnic negativity. It means no hunting for sport, no environmental misdeeds. No littering. No environmental or social negative impact made. The ramifications of respect stretch far and wide. From relationships to family, from the environment to cross-cultural reaches. And facilitating this respect is done through both action and inaction–active and passive responses.

"Passive respect would be *not* littering or not interfering in the life of another because you accept their behavior. Active respect would be picking up litter or planting a tree or helping another in some manner. Of course, these are very simplistic examples just to exemplify the idea, yet respect for all life brings a multitude of benefits. Most noticeable of these is the absence of negative attitudes toward others and the presence of a childlike wonderment over all the beautifully intricate facets of nature. This wonderment is born of an appreciation of the vitality of life itself and the awareness of its exquisiteness. This wonderment presents continual opportunities for discovery by revealing diverse ways in which all living forces thrive through their interconnectedness to each other. This unique wonderment brings clarity to the fact that this glorious interconnectedness of life is no small matter, that it has no confining bounds, but rather begins within self and expands outward like a pond ripple widening its circle out into infinity.

"A deep respect for life and the wonderment that accompanies it opens one's eyes to magnificent sights, it opens one's mind to nature's wisdom, where all species communicate through the common language of universal consciousness . . . The Knowing.

"An example of this would be the time I hiked over a barren hillside and came upon a lone flower growing between some rocks. Its unexpected presence startled me. I knelt down to admire its beauty, its tenacity. And following my act of expressed appreciation, I received its return response to me, the knowing that *one's true inner beauty doesn't require notice to thrive.* This tiny, fragile flower, full of sweet fragrance, grew strong and beautiful among rocks and barren soil. It said, '*I persevere despite adversity*' and '*I have the power to be me and I celebrate my individuality*!' These three expressions of wisdom came to mind as I knelt to admire the delicate life force before me. When I walked away, I had the distinct impression that the tiny flower felt some kind of an awareness of my appreciation . . . a connection of consciousness, one life force to another. And the communication exchange gave me an expansive fullness within my chest as I felt the magical enchantment of interrelatedness. This wasn't imagination or fantasy. It was a beautiful facet of reality."

Sally had an example of her own to reveal. "I seem to have some type of connection with hawks," she began. "So much so that I become concerned if I don't see one during a trip or journey. They'll fly over the road I'm traveling and I've come to take that as a good sign the trip will be a safe one. Do you remember when we went to town last month and the red-tail buzzed the car when we got down to the switchback?"

"How could I forget? We pulled onto the shoulder and got out to watch it while it literally danced in the air above our heads!"

"I'd never before experienced such a touchable communication from one of the hawks," she admitted with amazed remembrance. "I'd never witnessed one fly into a glide, invert itself, continue gliding upside down, then make a full upright rotation. Mary, that hawk played in the air right above our heads."

I smiled with the visual recall of the heart-pounding sight. "That was something, wasn't it."

"Didn't you feel it was expressing itself? It seemed to communicate a sense of shared joy."

"It was having fun. It said, '*Life is hard, yet there are reasons to rejoice!*'" I then glanced down at the tiny life curled in my lap. "Experiencing nature as I have—intently observing it—has verified the fact of interspecies communication for me. Noticing social behavior of the birds and animals underscored the existence of functioning intellects with transmission and reciprocal capabilities. Just observing how these little dogs so clearly communicate with us through their body language of posturing, their vocal variations and responses to our words, has brought me to a heightened realization that they really are little people—little people within their own species. They are so much more complex than being perceived as dumb animals."

My attention was drawn to the wall of bookshelves. "I have a wonderful book that depicts the intricate personalities and communication capabilities of animals. It's called *When Elephants Weep*. It brought a tear or two to my eyes when I read it, because it so clearly exemplified the reality of true *feelings*—emotional sensitivity—all living species possess. That's interconnectedness. That's *all our relations*. From the dancing hawk to the puppy desperately trying to get you to play ball, from the lone flower on a barren hillside to the brilliant, living coral, all life has consciousness and, through this vibrant consciousness, we are all connected. We are all affected by one another. We are all related through the beautiful, pulsating thread called Life.

"So then," I concluded, "we finally wrap up the qualities of wisdom's great power. Personal power is wisdom. The main qualities of wisdom are acceptance, patience, perseverance, silence, responsibility, individuality and the freedom of its expression, gentleness, priorities, understanding value, and respect for life by way of realizing its beautiful interconnectedness. These qualities instill incredible personal power . . . a gentle force that serenely rests within the garden of one's sacred beingness where, there, a strong muted heartbeat reflects its living power."

∞ ∞ ∞

"Wouldn't it be wonderful," Sally mused aloud, "if everyone understood what real power was? Society would be completely different because it'd reflect positive behavior. The collective consciousness of the entire world would be raised to a much higher and finer level."

"Mmmm, that's a beautiful thought, though a bit ambitious to realistically expect. What would open the door of probability for this would be for parents to teach their children what real power is. To learn at a young age that power is having the qualities of wisdom would turn an entire upcoming generation around. From that generation the possibilities greatly increase. Still, it's a long shot when considering how power is perceived throughout society. Look at the action films, for instance, where the hero is a muscle man wielding a gun as big as a rocket launcher. That impresses youngsters. They want to grow up to be just like their all-powerful hero."

"Children need better role models to emulate," Sally added. "But then that correlates with the adults who are drawn to the spiritual dazzle, doesn't it. If the adults are blinded by the glittery fantastic, then the children naturally follow suit. How can the youngsters be taught that the quiet and wise ones are the real heroes and heroines in life, when the adults don't recognize them as such? Oh my," she sighed with dismay, "this *would* be an ambitious task."

"Little by little, bit by bit, it could be done. Films could depict heroes and heroines with wisdom instead of with AK-47s. Children's books could do the same. Cartoons, video games, kid's Saturday morning television shows could all present heroes differently than they do today. All it takes is a bit of creativity. Little boys need to get away from believing power comes from a weapon-toting action hero and little girls need to get away from thinking power comes from the surface beauty of a glamorously attired doll with a teeny waist and exaggerated boobs."

Sally smirked at that.

"What," I shot back, "I can't call a spade a spade?"

Her palms went up. "Hey, you always do! Your terminology just struck me as funny, that's all. You're right, though. These kinds of toys foster the wrong ideologies for children. For boys, it's violence or war and the tools of both; in girls, it's instilling the subliminal idea that a perfect body and beauty are power—sexuality. Machismo and female sexuality . . . that's the current yin and yang perspective of power in the world. I don't know," she honestly admitted, "these ideas are ingrained so deeply that gentle men are viewed as weak, and strong, capable women are seen as unattractive."

"Beauty, in both men and women, is the wisdom within," I said.

"That's a fact." She paused before expressing deeper thoughts on the issue. "I think the problem stems from extremes. The glamour dolls and the power action figures represent extremes. Boys and girls need toys and figures to express themselves in play, act out roles. The problem is the *extreme* representation of these role-playing figures."

"That's a good observation. They should be moderated to accurately represent reality. Little girls wanting to be pretty is natural. Likewise, little boys wanting to imagine themselves having the ability to defend family and country is natural, too. Moderation is the key here. Toys geared to gender are important, yet they have to convey the right ideology. They . . . ."

Sally patiently waited for me to finish my thought.

I didn't.

"They what?" she prompted.

"Nothing."

"Nothing?"

"Well . . . when I was very young, maybe seven years old, I received a Madam Alexander doll for

Christmas. She had high heels and a blue taffeta dress. She was also probably the only doll of that time to have a tiny waist and breasts. I thought she was so beautiful until I caught my dad smirking as he showed it to his friend. That was the first of many events to follow from him that gave me the distinct impression that men thought women's bodies were laughable, or bad, or downright dirty. Consequently, I grew up with the belief, because I'd never been taught otherwise."

"God, Mary, that's awful."

"It's sad," I corrected. "It's pitiful. Anyway, I was well into adulthood before I realized how I'd been psychologically wronged, how every opportunity in my youth had been taken advantage of to ridicule my gender. Stupid. Subservient. Dirty. And the beautiful doll was left to gather dust on the shelf.

"There's a reason I'm recounting this. It's related to our issue. Now, of course, things are different for me. I love being who I am. I love all things associated with the feminine. I enjoy wearing makeup and donning long skirts. Now I celebrate my femininity, completely comfortable with my sexuality. Yet there also is the balance of perspective. There's a difference between loving who you are and *using* it. I don't perceive sexuality as power, but I see little girls growing up with that idea solidly formulating in their minds.

"The beautiful doll, with her perfect figure and beautiful clothes, her expensive possessions and upscale friends, all give the wrong impression of what real beauty and power is. These warp a child's view of value. They get 'in her face' with the wrong persona to strive to be when she grows up. Yes, toys have gone to the extreme. Many of them explain why society is the way it is today. We need action figures for boys that characterize heavy equipment operators, scientists, farmers, or dads. We need dolls for girls that depict airline pilots, surgeons, building contractors, and fire chiefs. Well," I sighed, "fat chance, huh."

My friend was dubious. "Maybe someday. Who knows."

"But why not now?" I reconsidered, with an unwillingness to let go of the issue. "Society has instilled the idea of gender-specific professions and the toymakers propagate it by continuing to define what type of hero our young people should revere and emulate each year. My own experience when young underscores how deeply impressionable children are. They need to realize how beautiful their individuality is, how uniquely wonderful they are. They need reinforcement of the fact that there are all kinds of heroes and heroines in life and that they can be so much more than a weapon-wielding superhero or a materialistic socialite living in her penthouse."

"It begins in the home," Sally said. "Parents are the child's first teachers and it's their role to continue to teach and advise until the child leaves home. If the parents are teaching right, then they're forced to be at odds with the toymakers and the cartoonists who create the heroes they flood the media and stores with. How do parents deal with such an overwhelming blitz? How do they comfortably deny their child the same action toys that every other kid on the block is playing with?"

Silence.

Waiting.

"I don't know. What I do know is that wisdom is the real power that people seek and the world will dramatically change for the better after the children also understand that. They need to realize that using gentleness and wisdom is far more powerful than using force and violence and sexuality to achieve success in life. Mental over the physical. The mind.

"The overall mind-set needs to be overturned. This is the main reason I wrote *Star Babies*. Because I've seen where the media is going with the issue of human beings from other planets, I needed to create a counter for the damaging negativity I saw being presented. When this issue was first presented in a grand way, through the films of *Close Encounters* and *E.T.*, I was encouraged to see that the perceptual view of such other-world human beings was one of intellectual acceptance and mutual benefit. Then the media took a downturn. The films that were produced after these became dark and violent. The mind-set was of fear and war. It generated the idea that all intelligent beings from other planets were bent on taking over or destroying earth and, of course, we, as the heroes, had to fight them off and save our dear planet from their evil invasions. You see . . . gentle and friendly isn't what theatergoers want. They want violence, suspense, thrilling explosions, and, most of all, they want their earthly ego stroked by being the planet that wins the day . . . the earth civilization proves more 'powerful' and is the victor."

Sally shook her head. "We even have managed to create a planetary ego. I can see now why you were so consumed with doing *Star Babies*. The current films generate *fear* of other planetary intelligences."

"Sure they do. It's the message society is giving to its children. I see it as encouraging racism. We perceive other planetary people as evil aliens. Are they not simply other children of God? Just because they may usually appear different in their physical appearance and advanced in their technology doesn't mean we must fear and destroy them. We have become a paranoid and fearful society. The beautiful 'difference' of people isn't celebrated and embraced; instead, it is viewed as being suspect and, therefore, must be evil and be weeded out. How sad. How incredibly sad and unspiritual we have become."

Sally looked at me. "*Star Babies* is a start . . . ."

"*Close Encounters* and *E.T.* were a start, but look what happened. All I can do is attempt to reach the wonderfully open minds of the children in the hope that they will view *all* human beings, no matter where they're from, as being God's children comprising the entire Family of God. We are all related." I sighed. "Overturning this mind-set could begin by stressing a child's specialness, his or her individuality and limitless imaginative creativity. Teaching children that their mind is their most powerful and versatile tool prompts them toward increased thought.

"Increasing conversational time by posing various 'What if' questions that will spark their natural curiosity gets them in the habit of thinking of possibilities they never before dreamed of. It heightens their problem-solving skills to where they'll learn that there isn't always just one solution or answer to a proposed scenario or question.

"I don't see evidence of a preponderance of plain old thought applied in society. When I talk about teaching children of the mind's power, I don't mean book learning, I mean plain logic and reasoning abilities. The power to think for self. Analyze. Children can do this with great skill. They do it quite naturally." I smiled then. "I'd been fooled a time or two when my girls were little more than toddlers. So, we know these children are highly capable of deductive skills at an early age; therefore, their minds are fertile ground to develop those powerful abilities. Parents can nurture this by posing hypothetical, simple scenarios or problems and helping the child think them out by guiding them through the process of passing from Point A to Point B to C. Logic puzzles and games are excellent practice activities that sharpen deductive talents. Learning to think for self can be fun. It can be accomplished without the child even realizing he or she is doing far more than just playing a game. Mazes are good tools that hone problem-solving skills. Games of observation are wonderful because they increase awareness. Teaching children to think and appreciate their individuality are two of the most valuable and powerful gifts a parent can give their children."

"Besides love," Sally added.

"That's a given."

"It should be," she concluded. "Anyway, I couldn't agree with you more about what you said. Learning to think for yourself—to reason things out—and having self-respect through a strong self-image gives a child a powerful jump-start in life."

"You know," I said, after musing upon my past, "although my father messed up my self-image when I was young, he at least encouraged me to think. He was always playing mind games with me."

"Mind games?" she questioned with a look of concern. "That phrase has a negative connotation in today's society."

"No, not that kind," I assured. "I mean *thinking* games of *logic*."

"Like what?"

"The one I recall most often is when he asked me this: 'Two men were working on a construction project. When they were done, the one with the clean face went and washed his face. The one with the dirty face didn't wash. Why?'"

"What was your answer?"

"What's yours?" I playfully responded.

She made a face. "I don't want to play. What was your answer?"

"They each thought their own face looked like the other's! The guy with the clean face saw his friend's dirty face, so he went and washed because he naturally assumed his was dirty, too. Vis-a-vis for the man with the dirty face who assumed his was as clean as his buddy's. Solving that riddle taught me a lot about *assuming* things."

Sally shook her head.

"These 'reasoning' games didn't begin until I was five," I said, "after something I did showed my dad that I had a brain.

"The family had returned home from a visit with friends and, upon turning the car into the driveway, I commented that the den light was on. We never left lights on in the house when we went out. Everyone else in the car said that it wasn't possible, that I must've seen a moonlight reflection on the window or something. Well, after we got in the house, I immediately raced into the den and then came back to my dad. 'It must've been a reflection after all,' I admitted to him. 'How do you know, Mote?' he asked. 'Because I felt the bulb and it wasn't hot.' His face lit up in surprise over my logical response. 'That's just what a policeman would've done!' he exclaimed. After that our mind games commenced in full swing."

"You actually went and felt the light bulb?"

"Yes, because finding the light off wasn't proof to me that it *hadn't* been on. The only way I could be assured was by its temperature."

"What was that name he called you?"

"Mote. I was little, like a mote of light. That was his nickname for me."

"A mote of light," she repeated.

"Maybe a dust mote," I said wryly. "I don't know. I no longer remember the reason. My point of the story is to emphasize the value of those mind games. When they're geared toward generating mental processing, they train the mind for a conditioned analytical response that comes quite naturally. This is the difference between asking a child questions that can be answered by going to reference books as opposed to asking questions that can only be answered by way of deductive logic and reason, whereby the mind is forced to think it out through a sequential process. This gets the child accustomed to thinking for self instead of running to others for answers. It fosters a reliance on one's own mind and also generates a fascination with solutions as it broadens one's view of the world of possibilities.

"Because of those continual mind games I played when young, I began to ask my own questions . . . of myself. An intense curiosity was sparked to life. Everywhere I looked I found a 'why' staring me in the face. I learned to ask questions of my own answers, to push further for more depth and then push at least once more. At an early age I learned that the answers I received from others weren't satisfying, that those answers weren't really answers at all . . . they were only varied opinions.

"Now I see people seeking answers from others. I see people asking everyone but themselves for answers. It's as though they don't realize they have a mind to think things through with and have no deductive skills to reason out their own inquiries. Is it laziness? The desire for a quick fix? Lack of responsibility or the fear of it?"

"It's all of the above and then some," she replied. "We've circled back to your issue of youth and what real power is. If the seeking adults were taught the power of wisdom when young, they wouldn't be asking every Tom, Dick, and Mary for their answers, would they?"

"I think we've exhausted our look at this subject. We keep returning to the children being the key."

"Amen."

At this point, a low growl rumbled out of Cheyenne.

"Not again," Sally groaned.

"Shhh, Cheyenne," I soothed while stroking her back. "Shhh, it's all right."

Her big dark eyes searched mine as if to question my surety.

"It's okay," I repeated.

After giving the shadowy room a good once-over, she scrambled beneath my chair. Things may have been okay with me, but she was heading for cover. This time the other dogs didn't share Cheyenne's nervousness. They remained undaunted, obviously oblivious to whatever had disturbed the larger dog's comfort zone.

For a few minutes we listened for a foreign sound.

Nothing was detected but the crackling fire and ticking clock.

My friend offered an alternate suggestion. "Maybe she was growling at something in her dream."

"Maybe," I said in a doubtful tone. "Maybe." Then thoughts shifted. "There's going to be evidence of religious intolerance showing up soon."

She was accustomed to my offhand statements coming out of the blue. "In what way? The public intolerant of a specific sect?"

"No. Religious sects being intolerant of the public, being intolerant of individuality and the expression of same."

My words were met with a questioning frown. "Certain religious sects have always been intolerant of those who don't adhere to their own self-delineated boundaries of behavior."

"It's going to accelerate to public denouncement by both group solidarity and individual activism. Crimes will be committed in defense of biblical concepts and the fanatics will perceive themselves as God's own appointed soldiers on a mission to cleanse humanity of the alleged infidels their twisted minds think they identify."

"Intolerance is not a spiritual attribute. Why can't they see that? What you're predicting will only show how they're going *against* God's laws and the teachings of Jesus. He had tolerance for everyone because he loved everyone."

"Yes. He loved their individuality. He loved to see people thinking for themselves and having the courage and conviction to follow their own instincts. He rejoiced in the diversity of life that surrounded all his many travels. The sights and sounds of the varied cultures he journeyed through filled his heart with excitement and warm enjoyment. Jesus celebrated life! He accepted everyone just the way they were.

"These religious sects don't follow that pattern. They act as though they are more holy. They don't follow his beautiful example of tolerance and acceptance; instead, they take on the role of God—that of judgment and condemnation. People are judged according to *their* specific beliefs. They are blind to their own sin of intolerance. They puff themselves up with false righteousness by pointing their fingers at others, while at the same time, they fail to see how their actions point their own fingers at self."

"Self-righteousness goes hand-in-hand with intolerance," Sally said, "at least most of the time."

"Most of the time it does. If you're intolerant you usually have a strong conviction that's at odds with the behavior or belief of another. The reason they're intolerant is because they're adamant that their way is right. So what we end up with is a self-righteous individual who cannot accept an alternate perspective. And *radical* self-righteousness *actively* condemns that alternate behavior or perspective. That's when it becomes dangerous and is an abomination in God's eyes."

Sally voiced an acceptable circumstance for intolerance. "Aside from the negativity of religious intolerance," she began, "everyone can be said to possess intolerance in some manner."

"That's true. Society as a whole has intolerance for rape and murder. We have an intolerance for incest and drunk drivers. Certainly there's a place for the line we draw that separates criminal behavior from that which is neutral and lawful. Yet this law-abiding behavior cannot be determined by the dogmatic strictures that bind a specific religious sect. To point a finger and chastise one of their own is their business. To point their fingers and publicly chastise *anyone* is not their business. That's intolerance. That's committing the sin of intolerance."

"That's the second time you've said that."

"Said what?"

"Sin. Isn't that term very Catholic or Christian?"

"My interpretation of the word is far broader in scope. It's not a parochial one. Sin, to me, defines negative behavior associated with *God's* laws as opposed to any specific religious sect's laws. Sinful acts are the acts that are contrary to spiritual behavior as outlined by the Ten Commandments. I don't mean sin to be synonymous with some kind of stain on one's soul, but rather *un*spiritual behavior. You know what?" I asked, changing the mood somewhat. "People really complicate their lives with intolerance. By making everyone else's behavior *their* concern, they miss the beauty of life itself. The old adage of 'live and let live' has lost its powerful impact. It's become a worn-out cliché grown meaningless through time. These words hold great power . . . if they're taken to heart and lived. Those simple words represent real spiritual simplicity to The Way."

"Know what?" she playfully responded. "It has occurred to me that your philosophy—your spiritual message—is not the simplistic basics you perceive it to be."

Now it was my turn to pose a frown.

"No. No, it's not," she concluded. "It's a full circle thing. It's the basics, yes. And, yes, it's spiritual truths to The Way in its most unadulterated, simplistic, and pure form, yet it's so much more. It's not merely Truth 101. It's not just a course in Spiritual Basics." She shook her head. "No. Your philosophy—your message—is not at kindergarten level at all, it's university professorship level, where acquired *wisdom* reduces it to simplistic beauty. *Wisdom* sorts out the superfluous and recognizes the power of spiritual simplicity. It's the wizened one who discovers this at the end of the long search. Wisdom brings spiritual value into a crystallized clarity of definition and focus."

I didn't immediately respond to her theory. I was thinking it over.

She waited for my opinion.

"Well," I said, "that's what I mean when I say 'going full circle.' A seeker begins with the basics and can't stop there. The seeker reads everything available and, as more and more in-depth research is fully processed, the inconsequential aspects are recognized as such and cast aside, leaving the jewels of knowledge to shine. Then the seeker adds these to experiential events and gains wisdom. What's left is the basics. Back to the beautiful simplicity–full circle. So, although the beginning basics are the same as the ending basics, those who have taken it full circle have gained valuable wisdom along the way. Their comprehension has great depth. Their basic truths are more precious."

"Is that necessarily so, though?"

"Clarify that."

"Well, you give your message of truth's simplicity. You tell people what's important and what's not. The archangel gave The Way on a silver platter. When folks accept this spiritual message with its simplicity, is it less precious to them because it was *revealed* instead of them gaining it through the long haul of self-discovery? Going full circle?"

"No, it's not less precious because The Knowing, even initially, brings people through experiential events of epiphanies. These serve as awakenings or breakthroughs that verify their beliefs. The wisdom comes on soft feet then. Step by gentle step wisdom enters one's field of understanding. Both ways are beautiful. What is gained is still precious. You know what I'm saying."

"Uh-huh, I do. It's only the difference of one spending personal research time and one initially recognizing the basics as being enough at the outset. One *working* through all the material and one *accepting* the simple truths from the beginning."

I nodded. "One gains wisdom *during* the searching process and the other gains wisdom by living the basics from the *start*. So, we're still talking about the truths being simple. Kindergarten or university professor, the basics are still the basics. Everything is still reduced down to the lowest common denominator, the wheat winnowed from the chaff."

"If the beginning basics are the same as the basics found after in-depth research is done, why go through all the searching to begin with?"

"You know the answer to that as well as I do. Some people *require* that searching process. They have a need to sort through and discover their own verifying elements. There are those who need more than the word of another. And that's okay. I'd rather they be sure than to harbor questions or doubts about what they've accepted. It's important for beliefs to be strong; convictions, solid."

∞ ∞ ∞

"So," she sighed, "any more predictions floating around in that head of yours?"

"Prediction? Is that what it is? I don't know. The mental visuals that come unbidden and the thoughts that I accept as a Knowing are precognitive events. They don't become predictions unless I voice them." My gaze shifted to the crackling fire. "What good are predictions anyway? The Time-Space Continuum is in a state of constant flux. Reality is like a beach that alters after the ebb and flow of every wave that passes over it. Each wave, a new probability that enters to alter the composition and design arrangement. The pattern is constantly changing. What I see at ten o'clock may be altered by ten-o-one."

"Then perhaps the religious intolerance won't come to pass."

"That's a solid one. The Knowing is too strong for that. Specific circumstances can change, but the varied events will still manifest in some manner. So will crimes be committed in God's name and for one's religious beliefs. These, too, will come about in time." I brightened then. "The one I particularly like is *books becoming valuable*. Books will become a precious commodity."

My friend shook her head. "You and your books. I've never seen anyone read as much as you do."

"I've always loved books. From the time I was a small child they've been like intimate friends. I love the feel of holding one while reading, the smell of the particular paper used and the ink of a new book, the flood of impressions that come with touching a very old book." I winked. "And you don't need electricity to gain knowledge from a book."

Sally caught the innuendo. "Books will be valuable when computers don't work."

"Worldwide computer viruses, magnetic interferences, and electrical outages . . . for long, extended periods, stealth from genius hackers. Books," I grinned, "books will be a valuable commodity, some as valuable as a gold bar.

"Also," I added, "computers will steal away everyone's privacy. Everything will be known about you through computers. Anyone will be able to access information on you. That's already starting to happen, isn't it?"

She agreed.

"Another couple of things that keep returning as a solid Knowing have to do with the medical arena and the insurance industry. The medical field will be in a state of great chaos one day and the insurance companies will fail, one after the other, like dominoes . . . no funds in their coffers."

"From? From being overwhelmed by exorbitant settlements. These being natural disasters," she rightly surmised.

"Yes."

"But the medical field, what specifically?"

"Politics. The public against the physician against the insurance carriers against the government against the health management companies. Chaos."

"See any good things?"

"Was that a joke?"

"No."

"Yeah. I see books becoming valuable."

"Was that a joke?"

"No, but there're good things, too. Like the cures for some diseases coming from botanicals . . . common ones. That's amusing to me because of the way the traditional medical field debunks the claims for healing herbs."

"What diseases?"

"Arthritis. Lyme disease. Lupus and immune deficiencies. Animals will also play roles in providing cures and effective treatments . . . animal parts, including fetuses and embryos. New techniques of gene therapy will eradicate many current-day diseases and afflictions."

"Anything else?"

"Yes. Oh, yes, there's more, but they don't feel solid enough to discuss. They keep altering a bit every time I get a visual."

"Colorado still a relatively secure place to be for the future?"

"The map in *Daybreak* remains unchanged. It's what was 'given' to me and it still holds true today. It will not alter its configuration."

She got sarcastic on me with a smart-mouth. A twinkle sparked in her eye. "Maybe you ought to market that map if probabilities won't alter it."

"You're awful! Why would I market it as long as people can look it up in their local library?"

"I know, I know. I was just kidding."

Cheyenne growled. It was a serious growl.

"Okay, everybody," Sally announced, while getting up from the love seat. "Outside!"

All the dogs raced to the back door as my friend mumbled, "I'm over this creepy growling bit. You dogs go out and bark at whatever spook you think you hear."

The door slammed shut in final emphasis.

I got up and stirred the glowing coals before lighting another cedar stick.

Sally busied herself in the kitchen and returned with fresh drinks. "Either something really has those dogs spooked or this place has got them imagining things. Cheyenne isn't usually like this."

I agreed. "She's normally nonchalant about the things that show up around here. She's usually pretty tolerant." Shrugging, I brushed the incident off. "Who knows, we all get jumpy at one time or another. Animals are no different."

After the little people came charging back inside, they were refreshed by the night air and wanted to play. They rummaged through their toy box and each chose a favorite item.

Sally, opting to sit cross-legged before the fire, inadvertently positioned herself in the center of the dogs' playing field and was immediately the recipient of stuffed animals, balls, and old socks. Accepting these simple invitations to play, she gave attention to each in turn while I watched in amusement from my chair.

After a time, Rosie and Punkin played tug with the sock.

Pinecone settled herself beside me and Baby curled up in Sally's lap.

Cheyenne stretched out on her side beneath my chair.

The activity wound down.

My friend stared pensively into the fire.

"What's on your mind?" I asked.

She looked over at me before facing the flames again. "I was thinking of perceptual variances, how people perceive an object, person, or event in so many different ways."

"What brought this on?"

"Nothing specific, more like a composite of various observations I've made over time. People perceive life according to their own unique set of attitudes and preconceived notions."

"Psychological makeup has a lot to do with that. Look at the old question: Is the glass half full or half empty? The pessimist sees it half empty while the optimist views it as half full."

"How do you see that glass?" came the unexpected response.

"That's not fair."

"Why not?"

"Because I'm one of those who scan a whole range of simultaneous perceptions."

"So? How do you see that glass?"

"I see it as being both half full and half empty. I also see it as being completely full and completely empty."

"So, you not only see the observable fact, you also envision the potentialities."

I nodded. "Want more? I also see it brand-new and I see it in the trash with a crack in it . . . its past and future.

"When we first walked into this cabin, I saw the observable facts of plywood floors, untaped drywall, bare windows, and no ceiling light fixtures. Yet I also clearly saw lustrous knotty pine paneling, forest green carpeting, cellular shades, and stained-glass light fixtures. When I observed no bathroom sink, I also saw a Victorian pedestal sink at the same time. When I observed no bathroom flooring or wall tile, I also saw green ceramic tiles and knotty-pine paneling. The real and the potential."

"Most people do that kind of envisioning when looking over houses to buy. They imagine how their furniture will be arranged and give thought to redecorating, yet there are also too many people who don't have that vision for potential. They would've walked in here and only have seen it unfinished and groaned at all the work it required. Yet your perception of that half-full glass surprised me."

"You were expecting to hear one of two answers instead of four or six. In fact, there could be more answers yet if someone responded by observing the *condition* of the glass instead of its content. This individual might say it's chipped or cracked, clean or dirty. All possible answers come from differentiating perspectives of relativity.

"Observable object, events, and behavior are processed through the filter of one's personal set of attitudes, whereby, the end product is colored accordingly. This is evidenced when multiple witnesses to a crime or accident give wildly conflicting statements. When one's perspective is tainted by past experiential events or by any of the 'isms,' such as racism, sexism, etc., you end up with *subjective relativism.*"

"Subjective relativism," she repeated. "Attitude interfering with objectivity." Turning the idea around in her head and examining it from different angles, she concluded, "It's not always a negative trait."

"No, it's not, yet it is something that should be thoroughly understood. It's why people see things differently. It's why folks need to understand that not everyone will see things as they do. It accounts for diversity of opinion on any given subject. It's why some people refuse to discuss religion and politics; those are futile issues of debate for someone holding strong convictions. Perspective is affected by beliefs."

"All right. And, your point is?"

"*My* point? You were the one to initiate this issue. What was *your* point in bringing it up?"

"Only as an observation of life. I imagine your point in expanding on it was that people need to understand the fact that others will see things differently than they do. Acceptance of another's opinion, kind of thing."

"Yes, but also a call for more objectivity, which is the opposing perspective of subjective relativism. Objectivity says: 'Look at the object, person, or event for what it *is* . . . just the observable facts as they stand on their *own* without any encumbering personal attitudes, opinions, or beliefs attached to them.' Objectivity says: 'Look at me with your *eyes* and not your opinionated mind!'"

Sally tossed a couple of small aspen branches onto the fire.

Glowing embers flared.

"So," she said, "much of reality is adulterated by judgments and opinions. Objectivity wants us to look at that half-filled glass without thinking that we don't like the shape of it or don't care for the color of liquid within it. Objectivity asks us to see the observable facts without opinion."

"Yes. It asks that our opinions and attitudes not be allowed to *alter* the facts. It asks us not to fracture reality into a thousand splintered fragments of perspective *before* it is first seen in its pure form."

"Like observing with nonthought–seeing what Is."

I smiled. "Just like that. Just like that because the 'real' of reality will otherwise never be seen. Otherwise reality becomes a personal world view comprised of opinions, prejudices, and attitudes.

"Objectivity allows us to step back and look at situations with clarity. We can do this when we reserve our knee-jerk reactions and opinionated responses. Looking at life objectively is much like having acceptance for what Is, at least it lets us *see* what Is.

"Remember when Robin invited us as her special guests to the seminar she'd just finished taking and the host asked the men in the audience to tell what they knew about women?"

"Don't remind me," came the disgusted reply. "They said women were gossipy. Women only cared about shopping and couldn't ever apply themselves to any sort of serious task."

"Uh-huh. And the women's responses about men were that they were lazy or all they cared about was beer and sports, or they were selfish and poor at following directions. What I observed was that not one respondent answered the host's question. He'd asked for examples of what is 'known' about the opposite sex . . . the *facts*. Everyone gave opinions, assumptions, and preconceived notions. Not a single person gave one fact about the opposite sex. And another thing that shocked me was the fact that all the answers were negatives! Where was respect for others? I heard no respectful answers!"

"What would you have said regarding what's knowable about men?"

"I would've said that they're all individuals with free wills, that they're all human beings, that they all have . . . well . . . noses! Those are *facts* about men as seen objectively without the baggage of any personal attitude interjected."

"Well, why didn't you raise your hand to give your answer, then?"

"Actually, I was just about to stand up to express how appalling all their negativity was to me when the host turned and began talking to the crowd. Sally," I exclaimed, "those people all gave *assumptions* as their answers! They didn't even *listen* to the question!"

"Hey, I was there, remember? People are so used to viewing life through the colors of their opinionated eyes that they no longer perceive life in an unobstructed manner. How else could those negative answers be explained?"

"And that's the second aspect that shocked me. Though the answers were opinions instead of the asked-for 'knowns,' not one opinion was a complimentary one. Though they were all personal assumptions, we still could've heard *positive* ones from the women, maybe something like, 'men like to handle the barbequing' or 'men make good car mechanics.' They could've given positive notions too, but they didn't. This simple seminar exercise gave proof that people's world view is perceived through subjective relativism instead of the clarity of objectivity. And," I emphasized, "this relativism is loaded with negativity. People are so weighted down with the clutter of negative notions that they make conflict resolution a near impossibility for themselves. The facts of life situations are clouded by their negative fog."

My friend was pensive. "People need to be responsible thinkers. Objectivity facilitates that."

"Responsibility, yes. Integrity of thought and perception."

"Mmmm. Integrity of thought," she echoed. "That's an interesting concept because it's been historically lost–irretrievably forgotten."

"It shouldn't be. It should be the natural norm instead of being the rare exception. It only seems 'interesting' because it *is* the exception. It asks folks to train their minds to see with objective clarity instead of attempting to peer through the muck of their assumptions and preconceived notions. This muck is thickened by associative emotional responses that serve to keep one entangled in the dark mire. Like quicksand, these emotions maintain a stronghold that prevents an individual from breaking free of negative thought. It holds one in a dark place where the clarity of objectivity never shines forth."

"Are you saying that objectivity is reached through the withholding of reactive responses? Emotional responses?"

"Only in a qualified manner, yes. Emotional responses are natural, yet those directly associated with assumptions rather than the facts need to be recognized and discarded, for these prevent clear perception of the truth of a matter.

"Anger, jealousy, prejudice, ego, etc., and the emotional responses associated with like negatives, twist true objective perception into a misshapened form. They're like dark, grotesque forms hanging around one's beingness. They're shadowy attachments to the mind. They're like dark clouds that never let the sunlight shine through—a dark and depressing world view." I sighed. "These are what a lot of unwise psychics identify as dark spirits being attached to someone. That's rubbish. It's nothing more than negative attitudes and opinions that need to be let go of.

"Objectivity is seeing everything in full sunlight. It's observing life without assumptions or preconceived speculations attached. It's watching life as it *Is*. Objectivity is beautiful in that it magnifies life through a crystal-clear lens of pure perception. Everything is seen in an untainted, undistorted manner—in pure form.

"Personal opinions add cluttered traits to that which is observed. For example, Jane Doe is being introduced to a gentleman she's never set eyes on before. She immediately begins a speedy mental processing, while outwardly being sociable. At the speed of light, she's mentally filtering this individual through her own strainer of perception. The preconceived judgment begins: *This man has a nose like my no-good Uncle Jake. His eyes seem shifty. He has a lisp like my former thieving business partner. His rings are pretentious, he must be an egomaniac. I don't like this character!* Done. Perception completed. This individual is shoved in the 'dislike' pile . . . just like that!"

Sally commented that it's a natural reaction for people to make corresponding associations between people when like physical characteristics are observed, yet she also recognized the futility and foolishness of transferring character to one from the other.

"But this is done all the time," I said, "because folks don't see objectively. Personal opinions cloud perception. That's not only unfair to others, it's also unfair to self. It stunts the growth of self and keeps one trapped in a stagnant state of being. It blocks personal integrity."

"The integrity of thought," my friend added. "Integrity of thought has to be well established before all other forms of integrity can manifest within self."

"That's a given, isn't it. We are what we think. Integrity is honesty. Honest thought comes from honest perception; honest in relation to the purity of objectivity–clear thinking that's without clutter."

I paused when I noticed she was deep in thought again. "What? What're you thinking?"

"The idea that 'first impressions' are so important to people. I was thinking about that. *Impressing* others is what it really means."

The firelight brightened her realization as much as it illumined the reflected sparkle of her eyes.

"First impressions," she continued, "are only important because society has a preconceived set of acceptable characteristics that judge people. That concept alone gives evidence of society's lack of objectivity. It says, 'dress and behave to impress others.' God, that's awful."

"It doesn't exactly promote individual expression, does it. It strikes a mark against the free thinkers who don't give a tinker's damn about impressing others. These types of individuals are then labeled as being nonconformists or eccentrics rather than being objectively perceived as individuals with the freedom to feel comfortable with their own unique beingness. As a people, humans are an opinionated lot."

A wry smile tipped my friend's mouth.

I grinned back in return. "What?"

"You were once caught in society's web of opinion."

"It's so pervasive it's almost insidious, isn't it. It wouldn't have happened if it weren't for my writings. Being a spiritual writer altered people's perception of me: one that bordered on holy or a sacred aura. Though I diligently emphasized my equal footing with them, they didn't hear or want to believe that I was no different from them. This was one of the reasons I shunned publicity and kept out of the public eye. Yet my readers' letters gave evidence that I wasn't being perceived as an equal and, though I still *felt* equal to everyone else, I also felt I couldn't do anything that could be perceived as lowering the value of my spiritual message. So, whenever a reader caught me playing video poker, I was so mortified I wanted to disappear down a hole in the floor."

"Your key word here is 'caught.' You felt caught

as though you were a little kid caught with your hand in the proverbial cookie jar."

"Yeah," I sheepishly admitted. "I did feel like that, despite the happy smiles and warm hugs I received from those people who recognized me; despite the fact that not one of them gave me any indication that I shouldn't be in that casino. What turned it around for me was the realization that I wasn't being true to myself. I either believed I was equal to everyone else or I believed their elevated perception of me. Well, that did it for sure. I knew I was equal, I was no holier than them. I scrubbed toilets, picked up dog doo, and folded laundry, too. My readers were in the casino and so was I. They were having fun and so was I."

Sally laughed. "How do you know what they were thinking? Instead of negative thoughts about you, maybe they were highly amused to see a visionary who likes playing video poker!"

I clicked my tongue at her. "Tsk-tsk, I'm no visionary . . . just me. Now I'm comfortable with being just me. And I like being just like my readers."

"What you did was maintain your integrity. You stayed true to your belief of being equal and didn't buy into any heightened persona others have of you. You walked your talk."

"Walked my *thought*, you mean. If you want to talk about integrity, then you have to associate it with one's *thoughts*, because not everyone's talk is the same as their thoughts."

"Lip service. External conformity while keeping one's opposing beliefs hidden."

I nodded. "Right. That's not integrity. That's not being true to self."

My friend got up off the floor and returned to her place on the love seat. "Mary," she began, "I just don't see much integrity out there anymore and I think it's because people really don't know themselves. Before integrity can be externally applied, it first has to be an active force within. I see too many people with wishy-washy attitudes–a lack of conviction, a lack of solid ideals. They don't know what they think and don't know what they don't think. Nor do they seem to care very much."

"That's when a hard look at self is in order. Know thyself. To *think* one knows oneself isn't good enough. This fits in with the objective relativism we talked about. Examining the whys and wherefores of one's attitudes and opinions should be a routine exercise to keep his or her objectivity in check.

"Where I notice this instability of thought most is in the realm of spiritual and new age concepts. There's no discernment applied. People seem to act like little kids in a new toy store, grabbing up everything off the shelves and heaping their carts full with whatever is new, shiny, and brightly colorful. Then they play around with all the new concepts and, eventually, have to possess every new spiritual toy that hits the market. No discernment. No solid convictions or integrity of thought applied because there's no *knowing* what one thinks. And the fact that this happens gives evidence of the extreme prevalence of fragmented thought and ever-shifting convictions."

Recalling a conversation I'd overheard exemplified my point. "When we were in the bookstore today, two women were examining the new age shelves. One lady pulled out three books and asked the other if she'd read them. They were all channeled works by various entities. The other woman was clearly nonplussed and not interested. Her friend rolled her eyes and commented in a demeaning manner, 'Really, Jane, you need to get up to speed on this stuff!'

"Here I observed one woman who had a discerning mind and had enough strength of conviction to know what was spiritually relevant and another woman who voraciously sought after it all without knowing her own mind. One had wisdom, the other thought 'being *up* on everything' was a sign of her high spiritual position. One had integrity, the other had verbiage and widespread knowledge of inconsequential matters. One knew self through self, the other knew self through a multitude of others.

"Another difference between the two women that I noticed was their aura condition. One was spiking and erratic. The other was smooth and calmly radiating. One felt desperate. The other felt serene. Knowing oneself and having confidence in convictions brings a deep inner serenity. There's no wild-eyed desperation to grab at everything new because, once one has The Knowing, *nothing* is new, all the *everything elses* are just so much irrelevant fluff not worth their time. Having integrity of thought is truly knowing self and, with that, comes an inner peacefulness that makes life an enchantment to experience. Life itself becomes an amazing wonderment. Love for God becomes All That Is for you. And all the allegedly 'new' new age material miserably pales in high contrast."

Sally commented that one needs to exercise critical and brutal honesty when examining the motives and thoughts of self. To really know self one has to control the strong urge to rationalize behavior and few could successfully do that.

I agreed, but with a qualification. "With routine practice, the rationalizations begin to weaken and fall away because you realize how often you keep fooling yourself, your own mind games become more and more evident over time and they become a bore. More and more you become conscious of that rationalized behavior and you begin to catch yourself in the act. Then you question self, 'Why am I doing this?' Realizing that you're only hurting yourself by not being true to self, behavior begins to turn around."

"You need a discerning conscience, though," she emphasized, "a scrupulous conscience. If one doesn't have scruples, he or she will always rationalize behavior."

"Probably. Yet routine self-examinations will also expose unscrupulous behavior. The trick for dispelling that is to get the individual interested in knowing self in the first place."

My thought-filled friend was silent.

"You were thinking of a specific individual here?"

"I loaned someone a considerable amount of money several years ago and, although I've tried contacting her about it, she avoids my attempts. She's making good money now, so I know she could at least pay something here and there. It's not even the money . . . it's the principle; no feeling of responsibility or obligation. No integrity."

"I appreciate your situation. You're not feeling bad over the money, per se, you're disappointed in your friend's lack of conscience. You'd feel better about it by accepting her behavior and writing off the loan by viewing it as a giveaway and letting it go. If she's avoiding you then she's attempting to avoid her obligations. You represent a conflict of conscience for her. Don't make her problem yours."

"I'm not. I only began thinking of her as an example of what we were talking about–integrity. Even in the business world there isn't much evidence of it. You yourself get told that the film option's check is in the mail or the contract revisions have been sent, yet three weeks later, you're still driving up to the post office looking for them. Then, when you find out that these documents are still sitting on someone's desk, you don't call them on the carpet for it."

"I can't undo their lack of efficiency, their forgetfulness."

"Your attitude makes you appear easy to take advantage of. You're naive."

"Naiveté is not the same as acceptance. I'm unconcerned about being naive regarding many worldly matters, but I accept behavioral characteristics that are generated by a lack of integrity. There's nothing I can do about it because it's a personal, internal issue that's unique to each individual's conscience. Maybe that attitude makes me look easy. Then again, I don't have to answer for their behavior either." I smiled then. "On the other hand, having acceptance for others' lack of integrity doesn't necessarily mean you *like* dealing with it."

My last comment tipped the corner of my friend's mouth. "Especially when you're expecting a check to pay bills piling up on your desk and that check's still sitting on someone else's desk."

"Sometimes it is touch and go, isn't it. That makes me no different than ninety percent of the population, who live week-to-week for their paychecks. So . . . back to the issue, I don't see my attitude as being any different than yours with your friend. Yes, you'd like to see her have more integrity and show responsibility regarding the debt she owes you, but you're not breathing down her neck for it, either. You've let it slide. Whether you consciously realize it or not, you have acceptance for her behavior."

No response came.

"And," I added, "like me, you don't particularly like that behavior."

"No. No, I don't. It's taking advantage of others. It's selfish and immature."

"The world is full of immaturity, but it won't always be that way. One day they'll be forced to realize what's really important. They'll have no choice in the matter, they'll grow up overnight. Well," I paused, realizing I was beginning to drift away from the subject, "Integrity means trustworthiness, doing what you say you'll do when you say you'll do it. It's dependability, honesty, and being able to be counted on. It's a strong sense of personal responsibility. It's knowing self with surety." And with that, the issue concluded, for no further comment on it came from across the room.

∞ ∞ ∞

Sally introduced a new subject by commenting on an odd incident that one of our mutual friends had experienced.

"Mary, remember when I took the autographed books to Victoria up at the casino last week?"

"Yes. You said she took a break to talk to you for a while."

"But did I tell you about the strange experience her husband had?"

A frown creased my brow. "No, I don't think so."

"Well, it seems that he and a friend were driving down a local road when they passed a woman gathering some sort of botanical from the open field. She was an Indian dressed in a traditional deerskin dress and had a basket to hold her newly harvested goods. The sight surprised both men and, after they passed her, they both looked back . . . she'd vanished.

When they asked another Indian woman about the incident, she told them to go back to the sighting spot and leave tobacco there for the restless spirit.

"The reason I thought about this now was our earlier experience with the buckboard. That wagon wasn't a restless or lost spirit and I don't think that the Indian woman was either. Wouldn't she be an imprint from a past time like the buckboard was? It appears to me that there are times and places where the veiled fabric of the dimensional curtain of the Time-Space Continuum is extremely fragile—thin, if you will—or seems to have a rent in it, thereby blending the past with the present."

"First of all," I said, "I'm sure Victoria's story gave this evening's sighting a bit more credence for you. These anomalies happen far more frequently than people think." I grinned with amusement. "They're a 'blast from the past' so to speak. Placing tobacco on the sighting spot has no effect whatsoever because the event is purely a matter of physics. Actually, doing that is rather primitive and ignorant of the reality of the situation.

"The so-called 'restless or lost spirit' idea has become a worn-out, catchall explanation for such manifested mechanisms of plain physics. The workings of reality are fascinating, to be sure, but we must understand them for what they are and not lose our heads over them by misidentifying them through false explanations of magic, supernatural, or esoteric causations.

"Folklore and many long-held traditional beliefs are proven out by our true understanding of quantum physics. What I mean is that the *events* and manifestations are proven out through our ever-expanding discoveries in physics, and these, in turn, dispel the folklore *causes*.

"There is no such animal as a 'supernatural' event. I've found all the explanatory answers relating to the causal factors of seemingly mystical manifestations by turning my focus to science. The natural process of my growth has led me in this direction and it's made all the so-called new age marvels of fluff settle neatly into a touchable reality of practicality. A *practical* reality comes into sharp focus when one delves deeper into the mechanizations of physics that keep our world working in an interrelated manner—the web of consciousness that interconnects All That Is, Was, and Will Be.

"Over the last few years, my excitement has grown over what the realm of scientific experimentation has exposed to the eyes of the formerly myopic scientists. Quantum reality suddenly made them face the fact that reality could no longer be confined within their staunch and unyielding laws that boxed in the pure mechanics of life; they now had paradoxes that confounded them. Yet those paradoxical events vanished completely when the added element of consciousness was factored in." My face lit up. "Yes. Yes! The Nobel-laureate physicists are now writing books on how this consciousness dispels the paradoxes that quantum physics once presented. The *scientists* are discovering that all of life is *interconnected!* Bravo! They are correlating quantum mechanics to the skills that mystics evidence! No more new age hoodoo. See what I'm saying? No more *super*natural anything . . . just simple reality. *Pure* reality."

My unrestrained animation had Sally grinning like a Cheshire cat. "You're really into this, aren't you."

"Well, yes! For years and years I've been frustrated over the rigidity of the scientific community. For years I've been saying that mysticism and psychic skills are just the pure workings of reality in its natural state; that it's *natural,* not 'super' natural. Now the physicists are seeing that it's true. Yes, it's very comforting to me. It's comforting because it'll lift many people out of the hocus-pocus mentality that had visionaries like No-Eyes raised up on some mystical pedestal instead of understanding that she, like many others of her kind, merely had a firm grasp of reality's physical workings. It was people's ignorance of the true physics of reality that caused them to view her in an awe-filled perception of mystic when, all the while, she was just doing what came quite naturally to her.

"My personal definition of the term 'new age' was 'the blend of physics and spirituality.' And one of the science books I read that was written by a physicist had a chapter titled *The Integration of Science and Spirituality.* You can't imagine how shocking that was for me to see. Shock and elation. I wanted to jump up and down, go running and laughing through the woods shouting, 'Yes! *Yes!*'"

Sally's smile widened. "Don't you think that the longstanding ideology of 'supernatural' came from not realizing that any seemingly mystical or psychic event was . . . Wait a minute, let me say this another way.

"If an event could occur, it was real and, anything that could happen was a facet of reality. Do you know what I'm saying?"

"Sure. The deal with scientists was a prior inability to equate the alleged supernatural manifestations to their then-believed limitations of the laws of physics. Now, due to the discovery of quantum expansion, they're no longer left scratching their heads.

"Eventually, I hope, the general public will likewise dissolve their limited confines of these natural events and cease to label them as being 'mystical' or 'powers' or whatever other terms repress their understanding of true reality.

"I'm overjoyed that physicists have now identified a solid explanation that unraveled their quantum conundrums. I'm tickled they concluded that *consciousness* plays a major role in uniting All That Is."

Baby rearranged herself on Sally's lap. "It sounds to me like this consciousness aspect would be connected to the mechanism of your *quantum* meditation. While you were talking about what the physicists discovered, I got a clear visual of the mind making quantum leaps through other dimensions—your onion-skin layers."

"It's going to take the mystery out of esoteric phenomenon and make it real. This has become a new age of science that will make the new age realm an age of New Science. We're getting closer to credibly interchanging the terms. The physicist and the mystic are finding out that they were on the same page all the while. They're discovering how much commonality they share. They're finally becoming friends."

"And you're elated over this."

"Let's say I view it as a giant step each has taken toward the other . . . a step that narrows the gap of ignorance that hung between them for too long. It's a beginning that's bright with sunlight."

"Maybe that beginning will continue to gain momentum in the right direction and the gap will be closed."

"Wouldn't that be something," I said. "We'll see. Maybe folks will finally stop being so amazed at the skills of their consciousness. When they accomplish one of these skills, they act like they just discovered fire! And organizations geared to helping people accomplish these natural skills are hailed as miracle institutions. We are a simple lot, aren't we?

"Physicists appear to have an ingrained fear of peering out into the unknown that lies beyond their identifiable and comfortable limits. Each advancing step they attempt is made with slow, tentative movements for fear their footfall will not land on solid ground. They have a fear of stretching out their arms to grope in the dark—to feel what lies beyond their brightly illumined knowables. We'll see."

"So you're not watching with bated breath."

"What, and suffocate? No, I don't watch or wait for anything with held breath. Each moment is accepted however it comes. The scientists' discovery of this consciousness element is enough to keep me going for a long time."

"You mentioned the fear that scientists have. Don't you think the very nature of their field warrants that caution. At least they *think* their work warrants it because their job is to define the boundaries of reality."

"There are no bounds to reality."

"They're working their way toward that realization, but until they get there, extreme caution is their law of the land. No scientist wants to be ostracized for making claims that go against the grain. None of them wants to experience peer humiliation or risk reputation."

"More the pity," I sighed. "Fear of reprisal, fear of being wrong or voicing an idea that contradicts popular belief didn't stop the claim of the world being round instead of flat. Fear is restrictive and represses potential. Fear conceals the beauty of daily blessings."

I rose from my chair to fuss with the woodstove. With the poker I stirred up the embers. Setting an aspen round over smaller branch sections, I replaced the screen and returned to my chair.

"Fear comes in many forms and touches lives in a multitude of ways," I said. "There's fear of failure, fear of not being accepted or not meeting the expectations of another."

Sally grabbed on to the last two examples. "Those are the fears stemming from ego. Those come from trying to impress others or live life according to another's set of values and attitudes."

"Being overly concerned with how others perceive you is not being true to self. What I see a lot of, and this is because of my specialized work, is fear of dark forces. This is a puzzlement to me because the brighter you shine with love for God, the greater is your confidence in God's protection. In fact, you get so illumined that thoughts of any dark forces never even come to mind. I reached that point a long time ago and found it wonderfully liberating. It sweeps away the dark shadows that make a murky perspective of life. I still had to deal with those around me who, through choice, remained obsessed with those fears, but for me, being free of them brought sunshine into every day, no matter how cloudy it tried to be. In order for life to have shadows it has to have light; which one you're drawn to focus on is up to you. You have that choice."

"What I can't understand," Sally said, "is why people don't see that. Well . . . I can see the causal factors they use, yet I don't understand *why* they use them. Do you know what I mean?"

I nodded and listened while she expressed her thoughts on the subject.

"Take fear of responsibility, for instance. That comes from fearing failure, not believing you have the wherewithal to carry your own weight—a lack of self-confidence. Why wouldn't you *want* to prove to yourself that you were a perfectly capable individual? Life is trial and error. That's how we learn from experience and do it better the next time. Nobody is successful at everything they attempt. Everyone messes up. So what! You pick up the pieces and try again. But to never try in the first place is like cowering in a corner within the shadows of your own fears. That's not living. That's not experiencing life and discovering your potential. That's choosing to be a wimp!"

That made me grin. "But, Sally, that wimp sees self as a success because there's never any failures to count. See? Confidence in self runs high because your 'wimp' keeps him or herself in a safe place by letting others shoulder the responsibility, the decisions and risk-taking lead."

"Then you're inferring that this individual is the follower throughout life."

"Not in all cases, yet this person usually isn't in the habit of thinking for self. The reason is self-evident—they want someone else to do the thinking for fear their own ideas would be wrong, not accepted, or ridiculed—fear of failure or humiliation. You see? We're right back to square one, no confidence in self."

My friend was shaking her head. "What about this fear of dark forces, then?"

"There's an interesting element to this particular one that's missing with all the other types of fears."

Sally's curiosity was sparked. "Wait a minute," she said, holding up her hand. "Let me think about this."

I waited no more than half a minute.

"The devil made me do it!" she proclaimed.

"That's what I'm seeing. People are using the dark side as a front—as an excuse for failure and as a reason to avoid personal responsibility. They're pinpointing the dark forces as a causal factor for all the negatives in their lives. By creating this handy scapegoat, they shift blame and responsibility to an obscure entity that, in turn, easily relieves them of culpability. Nice and neat, huh. All wrapped up in a tidy box with a big, black satin bow. Blame the dark side. Poor me."

"It's self-serving then."

"Sure it is. And convenient as all get out. No proof to the contrary for anyone to dispute."

"Except from someone who's spiritually aware enough to know otherwise," Sally interjected.

Her observation nudged a memory. "There was once a fundamentalist who befriended a member of my family. Whenever I was privy to their phone conversation, I continually heard this family member coo with syrupy sympathy and comfort over the other individual's cry of woe regarding her most recent 'satanic' attack. This person said she was 'attacked' several times a week! And I'd cringe to hear the cooing instead of the truth that I should've heard. You don't stroke people's delusions, you try to unearth the *reasons* for them. That woman was not being attacked, she sought sympathy for some other deep-seated psychological reason.

"Satanic attacks are just one aspect used. Sometimes they're used with this false reasoning: 'The more spiritual you are the more Satan goes after you.' Phooey!" I spat. "What a crock! That's as self-serving as you can get. That's supposed to announce to the world that the devil attacks you because you're so spiritual. Well . . . hello? Wake up, people, the *opposite* is true. Carrying the love for and of God in your heart lights you up like the sun! You're too much work for any sort of dark force to spend time on. To them you represent an impossible challenge. Yes, bad things happen to good people, but that's the natural order of life. That's not dark forces chasing you."

"There's a real obsessive paranoia out there about this. It's a serious phobia."

"Phobia. Yes, phobia. For years, every spring, I'd say to my young kids, 'this summer we'll all go to Elitche's,' which is a big amusement park in Denver. But when summer came I'd hear, 'we're not going to give the dark side an opportunity like that to harm the girls.' So we never went."

"Why didn't *you* take them, then?"

"I didn't want to cause discord so I let it go."

"Wasn't that stroking the delusion?"

"Probably. Yes, I see that now. It also probably instilled unnecessary fear into the kids' minds, too. Although, as adults now, I don't see evidence of that. They came to see that the idea was unique to one family member and made their own adjustments to it."

"Adjustments?"

I smiled. "One doesn't get the 'dark side' lecture if one doesn't announce her activities. Sarah would tell me she's going rock climbing or mountain biking with her boyfriend and I'd tell her to: 'have fun, be careful, and . . . don't tell your dad.' That's what I meant by 'adjustments' that can be made."

"Well, did you ever try to dissuade that dark-side obsession?"

"I talked and argued till I was blue in the face, totally frustrated with the situation. That's when I realized we needed to work around it and we began making those adjustments."

"Can I ask you something?"

"Sure."

"Previously, you've told me that you couldn't go on a cross-country autographing tour because some of those around you were afraid you'd be giving too many opportunities for the dark side to get to you. Why didn't you just go by yourself then if that's what you wanted to do?"

"I'm not a long-haul driver. On the interstates I can last maybe half an hour. Traffic bothers me too much to manage those kinds of distances by myself. I concentrate so hard on the driving that I wear myself out and need to take a rest. I needed a driver."

"Bummer."

"Yeah. Guess I'm a wimp driver."

"Now, now. That's not the same."

"I know. I do recognize areas I'm not skilled in, though. Long-distance driving is one of them. Anyway, too frequently I've seen this 'dark force' fear control people's lives. The reasons for it vary widely. What's sad is that the reasons aren't valid."

"You just said that, in essence, satanic attacks don't occur. Is that what you wanted to say?"

That gave me pause. "Yes," I replied after thinking it through. "Yes, that's what I intended to say. Without getting into explaining the true persona of this so-called Satan character, the differentiation between *internal* negativity and *external* negativity needs to be clarified."

"Wait a minute. We were talking about Satan—the satanic attacks."

"But our main issue is fear, the negativity that generates it and the negativity it causes. The concept of Satan is a separate topic altogether. By the way," I cryptically added, "Satan's gotten a bum rap."

"Oh," she sarcastically replied, "I suppose you're not going to explain that little comment."

"Maybe some other time. We're talking about fears and their negativity. But," I teasingly snuck in, "he's not the real Bogeyman."

"Mary!"

"What?"

"Would you stop that!?"

"Okay. Internal negativity stems from *within*. By that I mean internal psychological thought as applied not only to one's world view, but also to one's personal perception of self. And external negativity is someone *else* who affects us with his or her negativity from *without*. Most fears are generated from the first category and are exacerbated by the second.

"The greater the ego, the greater the fear. If you spend any time at all contemplating that statement, you'll see that it's true. What's to fear if one no longer prioritizes self? Even a fear that's thought to be noble, such as fearing the death of a loved one, ends up being self-centered because, when asked *why* this is a fear, all the 'I's' come forward."

Sally heard what I was saying. "'*I* will miss you. *I* will be all alone. *I* will have no one to love. *I* will be heartbroken.'"

"Yes. Instead, one should be glad his or her loved one is back with God, back to where there is no physical pain and suffering. Death is not an exit, it's an entrance. We fear another's death because we can't resist associating it with the sorrow and pain of heart we don't want self to experience. There are few bona fide, true fears."

"You have a fear of flying," she stated.

"I used to believe that, too, until I analyzed it. Nobody can fear an experience that will never be experientially manifested. I vowed to never fly out of respect for a past warning premonition. Therefore, how can I fear that which I'll never do? That's like saying that I fear doing brain surgery. If I were a neurosurgeon that might be true. Also, fears are often confused with anxiety and concern. These don't necessarily define a fear.

"Getting back to negativity, we see that most fears grow from the negative ego-based soil conditions of the mind. Fears of rejection, humiliation, failure, responsibility, etc., come from a desire to impress others with the fine, successful, and admired character of self. There is a pride involved here, a personal pride associated with being accepted, admired, and even well-liked by everyone. Ego. Control is a fear-based desire. Of course, by 'control' I don't mean self-control, I mean the manipulation of others–dominance.

"The fear of not being accepted or well-liked by everyone isn't even rational. It's not rational because of the subjective relativism we discussed earlier. Every individual perceives differently. Even God has Her detractors. When negative psychological ploys are implemented to shield the ego, fears abound. Lacking self-confidence is egocentric because it says, 'I don't want to embarrass myself' or 'I don't want to look stupid' or whatever. Self-confidence is the *positive* side of the coin that is not egocentric. It says, 'Win or lose I'm going to try my best,' or 'Whether I fix this or mess it up, I need to at least make an attempt.'

"Gentle self-confidence doesn't guarantee success, it guarantees the freedom to express self, to go for the gold, to experience successes and failures alike without fearing failure or the opinions of others. Then, of course, there's over-confidence, which is the cockiness where action is taken before thoughtful planning is applied. An 'I can do anything' mind-set is all right to have as long as cautious thought is utilized along with it. Over-confidence has the distinction of possessing positive and negative polarity and thought, the application or lack thereof, is the determining element."

"Fear of the future is a major issue right now for many people," Sally commented. "I know you touched on this subject already, but since we're discussing fear, I thought I'd bring it up again."

"Fear of the future comes from not having acceptance of reality and also exposes a lack of confidence in God's love for us. It's so important to stay focused on the moment; to live for today so the gift of life can be appreciated and lived to the fullest. If that appreciation for today isn't realized, what would it matter what tomorrow brings? See what I mean? If joys aren't felt and blessings aren't counted on a daily basis, then the tomorrows are going to be just as bland and joyless anyway.

"A fear of tomorrow won't alter what tomorrow brings. Fears don't change anything, but maybe they give you ulcers. On the other hand, acceptance keeps one on a more stable, even keel of balance that stabilizes the yaw toward negative attitudes and emotions. I can't stress enough how peaceful one becomes when he or she sees the incredible beauty that exists in life. Why anyone would want to disrupt that peacefulness and wonderment with fear is beyond me. Appreciate the life of Life every moment of the day; tomorrow will always take care of itself. The most beautiful way to live is to remember that today may be the last day of your life. By doing that we find ourselves loving more, accepting more, and appreciating the beauty of something as simple as sunrays backlighting a flower petal. This ideal accentuates our kinder side and highlights the futility of negative emotions such as anger, resentment, or jealousy. It brings forth an enchanting appreciation of every hour you're given. Fear of tomorrow steals away the gift of today.

"When thoughts of tomorrow come to mind, they should be thoughts of Possibilities—possibility for opportunities and additional joys and blessings to experience and treasure. Every additional day we're given is an opportunity to make needed retributions or exercise unconditional goodness. There're unlimited ways we can make productive use of the new day we're given if it's perceived as a blessing, as a gift of possibilities. Daybreak . . . the Creator illuminating Her gift of Life. How can such a golden gift be feared?"

"It seems to me," Sally mused, "that some people have managed to wedge themselves between a rock and a hard place. They fear the *living* of their tomorrow and they also fear death. No wonder they're so unhappy with their existence. If they're not appreciating God's gift of life each day, then they only exist—like a zombie—their spirits are already half dead."

"One's spirit cannot be confused with one's physical, mechanical mental state. The spirit is always and forever a vibrant force within one. Aberrant psychological manifestations do not affect the ever-shimmering spirit or its vitality. To say someone's 'spirit is broken' is a grave misnomer."

"Then people's depressive *mood* and negative *thoughts* make them half dead, in that they find no joy or appreciation of God's gift of life."

"That's a more accurate statement."

"So they fear the living of each dark day ahead and they fear death, too."

"A very shadowy place to voluntarily position oneself, I'd say."

"Especially when death isn't even something to fear."

"Death is relative to individual thought," I reminded. "The only way it could be perceived as fearful would be if it were considered by someone who believes in a fiery afterlife place and is also leading an absolutely negative life." I smiled. "That would be scary. However, there is no fiery place.

"The atheists believe there's nothing; you die and you're gone—poof—no more existence anywhere. So, what's to fear about that concept? Those who believe in St. Peter's pearly gates have something to look forward to. Those who believe in the Light at the end of the tunnel can rejoice in the thought of taking that beautiful journey. Where's the cause for fear?"

"Doubts," my friend replied. "A lack of conviction. The pearly gates, the Light, and even the *nothingness* of the atheists are nothing to fear if one strongly believes one of those afterlife scenarios is true. Fear creeps in when a shred of doubt exists. Also, people believe that death is a journey one takes alone. You can't bring along a friend for moral support."

"I agree with your 'doubt' factor, but let's look at the 'alone' thing. The atheist isn't concerned with this because there's no *anywhere* to travel to in their minds. The rest who believe in the spirit's afterlife journey don't take that trip alone. Those spirits are immediately met by angels or passed-on loved ones or other spiritual entities one identifies with. They are accompanied by loving entities right from the start. Death is not a lonely transition."

"A lot of people are going to take comfort in that fact."

"And well they should. There's no reason not to. Like life, death can be a beautiful experience."

Sally made no further comment and I had nothing more to say on the subject.

∞ ∞ ∞

I added my voice to that of the snapping fire. "Did I tell you that I . . . ."

A movement on the porch caught my attention. "There's a big dog on . . . oh, my god!" I whispered, "there's a *bear* on the porch!"

I eased myself off the chair and quietly climbed onto the cedar chest beneath the window while Sally cautiously crossed the room. Silently we watched the black bear as she licked up the sunflower seeds and breadcrumbs scattered on the porch. Like a living vacuum, she moved along with nose to the ground. She was so quiet (and the generator was running, too), that the dogs heard nothing.

My heart was drumming as I watched the great mass of fur advance toward us. When she was directly below the window ledge, her head popped up.

Startled by my eyes catching the bright moonlight, she sat up and slammed her great paws on the window ledge.

My heart stopped.

The bear and I were nose to nose with only fragile glass between us.

Sally grabbed the back of my blouse and yanked me back into the room.

The bear scrambled down the porch steps.

Sally ran for the gun.

The dogs were now barking up a wild storm.

Gunfire shattered the night's stillness and the four Yorkies leaped into my lap. They were trembling from the noise.

Sally came back inside. "I shot into the embankment. The noise kept her going," she announced. "I could hear her running quite a ways through the woods."

After reloading, she placed the gun on her couch-side table and released a deep sigh. "You okay?"

"Yeah. Wasn't that *awesome*!"

"Awesome! Jesus, Mary, she could've come right through that glass at you! She looked up and saw your eyes. You startled the shit out of her. You were damn lucky she ran instead of going for you!"

"I didn't count on her looking up. She was so intent on eating that I forgot that the moonlight would've reflected in my eyes."

My friend was so upset over the incident, she paced before the woodstove. The amber firelight did nothing in the way of illuminating the greater lights of her sparking aura.

"Mary?" she spouted in irritation. "Shit! A *bear* nearly came through that window! A *bear!* Do you realize what a mess . . . Do you realize what could've . . . ."

"Sally," I smiled, "you're not in Kansas anymore. This is the mountains. You're in bear, coyote, and cougar country now."

Her pacing slowed a bit. "Well, no . . . shit!" Her eyes locked on mine. "You think this is funny? Do you even realize you were nose to nose with a friggin' *bear*?"

"It did happen pretty fast, didn't it? No, I don't think it's funny. When she made that pounce with her paws my heart lunged, felt like it popped clear out of my chest. I've never been nose to nose with a bear before. It was a blessing the way it ran off like that."

"*Some*body is sure watching out for you!" She eyed the window. "Close those drapes."

"No. I like sitting here and looking out at the valley moonlight, seeing all the stars. How many times has a bear come up on the porch? It's not like it's a nightly event."

"Once is enough."

"It'll happen again," I said. "They're just looking for food, that's all."

"You've got critter food all over this place: alfalfa and grain for the elk, seed for the birds, corn for the squirrels and chippers, and salad for the rabbits.

For God's sake, you even put out cat food for the stray cats! Jeez, Mary, all the critters know this place as Rain's Diner!"

"What," I said, "I'm supposed to close down the diner now? I don't think so. Besides," I conveniently reminded, "the cans of cat food were your idea. You felt sorry for all the pets people bring up into the mountains to abandon. Who brings home lost dogs? Who has a bird cage on the porch to use as a 'recovery room' for the birds that hit the windows and stun themselves? Huh?"

"Well . . . ." she grinned, "that's different."

"Is it?"

She plopped down on the sofa. "I guess not. But . . . a bear!"

"Yeah, a bear. Too many critters have come to depend on us for food to take it all away from them. We'll deal with it. I don't think it'll want to hear the noise of gunfire too often. Do you?"

"I wouldn't think so, then again," she reminded, "how would I know, I'm a Flatlander."

"Not any more you're not." I inclined my head to indicate Baby. "You and Toto there are definitely not in Kansas anymore. Not only have you entered the world of 'wild things,' you've also come up in the world."

"I like living at ten thousand feet," she pleasingly responded, "you don't swelter in the summer and the clouds hang down in the valleys. The nights are incredible; I've never seen so many stars in my life. It's a magical place to be. Well . . . what's really amazing is the fact that it's real—the magical sense of enchantment comes from the real of it all."

Her joy of wonderment gladdened my heart.

She was no longer upset over the bear incident.

"The only thing wrong with Colorado is that there're too many people moving here."

"You did. And, over twenty years ago, I did too. Seems most everyone here came from someplace else. Ever see the bumper stickers?"

"Bumper stickers? You mean the ones that look like Colorado license plates that say 'Native?'"

I nodded. "Those announce the people who were born here, they're proud to be a Colorado native. You ever seen the others?"

"What others?"

"There's one that says 'Semi-Native' and one that says 'Transplant.' I guess you're considered a 'transplant' until you've lived here for twenty years or so."

"So I'm a transplant and you're a semi-native."

I shrugged. "This is my home. That's all I know. Never did care much for labels."

"I think it's silly."

"Me, too. There're a lot of people who take it very seriously, though. There's a feeling of deep pride the residents have for this state. It says a lot for the awe-inspiring natural beauty found here and the people's appreciation of it."

"Well, yes," she conceded. "By the way, what were you starting to say before the bear came?"

"Oh! I wanted to tell you that I counted thirty-one ring-necked doves yesterday. Fourteen of them were on the porch, seven of them crammed on the squirrel feeder."

"That's more than I counted last week. Word must be getting around about this place. They were all perched like vultures on the bare branches of those dead aspens out front. Hey," she exclaimed, "guess who I saw sitting on the split-rail fence by the drive?"

"The owls?"

"No, mama grouse! Her young ones were moving around in the tall grasses beneath her."

I expressed surprise to hear that our grouse family had ventured so near the house because the generator noise and dogs in the yard certainly seemed like things the mama would want to avoid. "You think all the doves hanging around made her feel more comfortable?"

"Could be. This place is crawling with wildlife, Mary. Just about the only critters we haven't seen here yet are cougars and raccoons." With a pensive tone, she said, "I miss Rocky and his girlfriend." (A pair of raccoons Sally hand-fed at my former stone cabin.)

"I don't doubt raccoons are all over in these woods somewhere. They just haven't introduced themselves yet."

"Rocky liked apples and my chocolate chip cookies. Maybe I ought to do some baking."

My lower jaw dropped open. "No way! We've got to stop feeding the critters, remember?"

"Okay, touché. Ever see any cougars?"

"When I lived up on top of the Dandy Jim Drive road in Cripple Creek Mountain Estates. You know, where all the bighorn sheep gathered in the yard. I was once at the kitchen sink and, when I looked out the window, I caught the back end of a cougar disappearing over the rocky ridge. The long tail was unmistakable. I didn't care for where that house was situated. It had a breath-taking view, but it was far too rocky and barren for me. No woods."

"Why'd you buy it then?"

"Bill loved it."

Sally didn't want to expand on that. She didn't want to go there. Instead, she brought the conversation back to wildlife. "I wish we had deer families coming here like they came at your little cabin. Watching them feed and interact kept us entertained all evening. We haven't seen much deer or elk here."

"That's odd, isn't it. Especially since the former owners told us about the elk herds that graze down in the valley. Do you think our noisy generator scares them away?"

"Didn't seem to bother the doe you saw browsing the weeds out front. Didn't bother that young buck we watched mosey along the back fence a couple of days ago. Maybe their seasonal movements are different this year, because the old guy down the road also mentioned elk in this valley. I think we need to be patient. Hey!" she perked up. "I saw what you did the other day!"

I frowned. "What'd I do now?"

"On the porch, that little pine siskin you walked up to. I saw you pet it!"

My eyes brightened. "Oh yeah! That was so incredible! It just sat on the railing while I stroked its head and back. Then it flew into the spruce. Gosh, I'd love to see the day when I can sit in the woods and have all the critters come up to be petted. Wouldn't that be something!"

Sally tilted her head and eyed me with an incredulous look.

"What?" I asked.

"You don't have a clue, do you."

"About what?"

She rolled her eyes. "Nothing. Nothing, Mary."

"What?"

"Things happen around you. Things that are an amazement to me happen around you and I am blown away that you don't see them as anything other than normal. Things that have become routinely 'normal' and natural to you are an amazement to others."

"Nuh-uh," I denied. "Like what?"

"Like what? I'll tell you like what. Like those two pair of owls that came and greeted you the first evening we were here. Dusk, remember how they buzzed over you then perched right up there in the aspen branch and talked to you?"

"Us. You were out there, too. They talked to *us*."

Her head was shaking. "You also going to deny they weren't real owls?"

"I don't want to go there. What else?"

"That was a slippery answer. What else? That *light* that came from you that night. The altered *facial* features I see on you when you're meditating. Petting a wild bird. Hearing *footfalls* across the carpet when there's nobody *visible* making them. Seeing *movement* behind you in the evenings. A friggin' *bear* that runs instead of instinctively attacking someone who startles it at nose-to-nose range! Jesus, Mary, the examples are endless. Want me to go on? The *wings* I see reflected on the windshield when I'm driving . . . ."

"Okay. Okay!"

"Well?"

"Well what? So you notice things." I grabbed the woolen shawl from the back of my wing chair. "I'm going outside, wanna come?"

Leaving the dogs inside, my friend reached for a jacket from the wall peg and joined me on the porch. Sitting in the cypress rockers, we were silent for a time.

The heavens sparkled like sun on glittering new-fallen snow. Diamonds, rubies, and emeralds rained down their riches through the silvered light of the moon. Such richness. Such treasure for the eye to behold. It made me feel wealthy beyond imagining and I fought the longing to run down into the valley.

"I didn't mean to cut you off in there," I whispered.

"I know. It's beautiful out here, isn't it."

"Yes. So beautiful."

"The bear's gone."

A smile tipped the corners of my mouth. "Bear's gone."

I heard her release a quieted sigh.

"Bear's gone," I repeated, "but kitty's here."

"Where?"

"Creeping toward the stairs."

In a flash my friend raced back inside, only to reappear with an opened can of cat food.

"I forgot to put it out earlier," she said. "Here, kitty-kitty!"

The kitty scampered away in retreat up the drive.

The food was set on the ground.

Coming back up the stairs, Sally confidently announced, "She'll get it later."

Our chairs rocked in a quiet hush over the weathered porch boards. After a time, I broke the metered sound. "Sitting out here like this, you can almost feel the great Web of Life, can't you. The great lights of heaven shining down on this valley—on us—touching There to Here, makes me feel as though I'd make a vibration along a strand of that Web if I so much as blinked an eye. So delicate. So fragile, yet bearing the strength of silken threads. The consciousness of All That Is binds and entwines us all together in one breathing entity of beingness."

"You're waxing philosophical again."

"Mmmm. Can you feel it though? Can you *feel* the Web vibrating with the movements and thoughts of life? With the thriving life force of everything?

"Look! A falling star!" I exclaimed, pointing to the descending arc of light. "How incredibly grand it all is, so unimaginably massive, yet all connected to the consciousness of the One.

"The Nobel-laureate physicists I spoke about before were excited to discover that the presence of a consciousness was the determining reason that explained how one electron could have an effect on other electrons from a distance. That singular breakthrough demonstrated the interrelatedness that exists between all the components that make up reality. The feeling I had of that lone flower's awareness of my presence and subsequent admiration of its beauty and tenacity is explained through the physicists' epiphany. Science has finally found its own validation for events once relegated to the esoteric realm of highly skeptical possibilities.

"Your own connectedness to hawks manifest through the same principle. Your consciousness and theirs lock onto each other. There's a linkage that occurs . . . a magnificent, living connection."

Sally expanded on the idea. "This consciousness factor explains why plants thrive by responding to a serene or happy atmosphere, why they do far better when they're tended to with love, and the noticeable effect music has on them." The moonlight glinted in her eye when she turned to face me with a smile. "Maybe now some people won't think it strange to see someone hugging a tree."

I chuckled. "Well there are still more than a few folks who'd raise an eyebrow to see the way I pet my plants. Soothing their leaves and talking sweetly to my greenery would still seem like oddball behavior."

"Only to those who aren't aware of how far science has come." She scanned the heavens. "God, Mary, isn't this incredible. Wouldn't it be fun to put skylights in our bedrooms?"

I didn't need to give that one much thought. "No. I definitely wouldn't want one over my bed."

Her frown vanished as quickly as it appeared. "Oh,

I get it. You think you'd spy those little Starborn peeking down at you."

"You may think that's very amusing, but those kinds of thoughts come naturally and instinctively after one has had several encounters with them."

"My inclination is to take that farther," she said. "They don't need skylights to peek at you if that's what they want to do. They'd just manifest *in* your room."

"That's true, yet those skylights would still give me an uncomfortable, nerky feeling. I suppose this whole thing would be a bit hard to understand unless you've had encounters, too."

"Oh, I can understand it. I've had plenty tastes of the feeling you're referring to when I stay up late to paint. Feeling as though someone's standing behind me, noises I can't identify, sudden breezes, and movements caught out of the corner of my eye that make the dogs growl under their breath can be unnerving. Still, a skylight would be interesting, I think."

The underbrush below the porch rustled.

"Kitty won't come close enough to eat if we're out here," Sally whispered. "Let's go back in."

We quietly rose from our chairs and tiptoed back inside. We were met by wagging tails and whimpers of gladness. The little ones' enthusiastic expressions of love never passed unnoticed, for their affectionate ways always tickled my heart. It felt so, so good to be loved.

After reciprocating the little ones' affection, Sally went into the kitchen to refresh our drinks while I took care of the woodstove and lit another incense stick.

Handing me a cup of steaming green tea, she commented, "When I talked with Ken at Hampton

Roads yesterday, he said they'd been getting some negative reader response regarding *Bittersweet.* Seems some people don't want to read about your problems."

No comment.

"Does that upset you?"

"*Bittersweet* was two books back. No, it doesn't bother me. There will be as many different opinions about my books as there are people. My correspondents continually ask me what's going on in my life and I gave them a book with that detailed information. The content of *Bittersweet* paralleled events that many of my women readers were also experiencing and it gave them encouragement to persevere and do something about their own situation. Other readers only want 'sweetness and light,' like the lady who didn't buy the dream book because she wanted me to get back to writing magical stories."

"If I recall," Sally remembered, "she said she wanted stories about fairies and happy, woodsy experiences."

"She wants fairy tales instead of reality. She needs to buy her books from the children's section.

"*Bittersweet* helped a lot of women. Those who don't like it are missing the whole point of it. That book was written for two reasons: to show people that I experience the same trials they go through in life and that they too can persevere, and the second reason was to conclude the *Soul Sounds* journal—a conclusion defining the transitional period that accelerated spiritual and philosophical growth. Through *Bittersweet,* people saw that spiritual messengers are no different from them, in that we are all existing on equal human footing while walking this earthly realm; that, through adversity, we can become stronger, learn and grow. I'm not here to write fairy tales. I'm known for calling a spade a spade and it's my nature to do so. If people want something other than that they need to be reading another author. Life is serious business, too serious to waste anyone's time in their search for answers or cries for help."

"So those negative letters don't bother you?"

"Expressed opinions show where people are at. Everyone is at a different place with their level of perception, reason, and degree of understanding. I recognize and accept that varied placement. What's interesting is that there's usually some personal hidden issue or agenda in a person's own life that prompts such negative responses. That's what really needs to be recognized and addressed. Instead, they transfer their feelings to an external scapegoat. It happens all the time and people aren't even aware that they're doing it." I smiled. "People's positive letters warm my heart and give me encouragement; the negative ones are accepted with complete neutrality."

"I don't think I could do that," my friend admitted.

"Yes you could. You could and you would."

Sally decided not to argue our different perspectives on the issue. "Going past whatever my own reactions would be, I see the negative letters as not only relating to the correspondent's level of understanding but also revealing a coarse aspect. Know what I mean? Some letters are downright hostile and full of explosive anger."

"Impoliteness," I said. "They're impolite. They say things that are rude and hurtful, thoughtless things I wouldn't dream of uttering to another. Yes, some do expose an extremely coarse aspect of their personality. Rudeness doesn't reside within a spiritually aware individual because that's where acceptance and the wisdom of silence would automatically take over. The wise one checks a knee-jerk response of rudeness with silence and goes forward without letting the incident affect him or her. There's a lot of rudeness out there right now. Any driver can tell you that. It's so prevalent that they created a term for it. Road rage is everywhere.

"The joy is stolen from Christmas shopping by the push-'n'-shove crowds. People say terrible things to each other without remorse because they feel no guilt over it. It goes back to ego. '*I'm going to say what I think whether I hurt your feelings or not*!' No thought given to others . . . only to self. Rudeness is self-gratification for those who lack acceptance.

"You know," I said, "there have been times when I've been tempted to make a response but held my tongue because I felt that maybe my words could've been interpreted as being rude. Specifically, this happens whenever someone asks me if I've read a book by this channeler or that one. I want to say, 'What for? I'm perfectly comfortable with my relationship with God, so why would I be interested in hearing something from anyone else?' See? I want to state my personal position, yet feel it may be translated as a sarcastic remark so, instead, I tell them I haven't heard of so-and-so and then patiently listen to their adulating diatribe without giving further comment."

"You're perfectly within your right to express your opinion or state your position," Sally said.

"Am I? That's not how I see it."

"Everyone has a right to an opinion, even you."

"That's true, but because of how many people take my opinion as fact, I have to always be discerning in what I say and how it's said. Oftentimes I have to withhold heartfelt sentiments and private thoughts because of the fact that, if expressed, people take them as being some type of directive. That happened when I recounted the conversation with the archangel in *The Visitation*. I expressed my heartfelt feelings and there were those who took great offense.

"I'm comfortable making *general* statements, yet I'd never publicly comment on a *specific* book title or author; I always respond by telling the person that they have to go by how *they* feel inside about these.

"My god, Sally, people want me to be their personal literary judge when that's *their* responsibility. So, though I give general guidelines, I carefully watch what I say. If John Doe thinks some new channeled entity is the greatest spiritual voice since Moses, then so be it, because that's where John Doe is at in his searching development. Who am I to disrupt that course? I'm not the Church here to stamp book titles or authors with its imprimatur. I'm not here to tell people what not to read. On the contrary, if one is still searching, then I enthusiastically encourage them to read and read and read some more. Not just the new age subjects, though. Read and study science, physics, the gnostic gospels, and the historical philosophers and scholarly texts, for they are all interconnected and lead one as through a tunnel to the ultimate reality."

I could see Sally's mental gears turning as I spoke. Her response was a natural extension of my words. "Well then, when people ask you if you'd read so-'n'-so, you could respond by asking them if *they'd* read this book or that one."

"I could . . . ."

"You're hesitating."

"I'm hesitating because whatever book I might suggest may not be one they're ready for. Depending on where their development is and where their intellectual level is, my suggestion could ultimately be beyond their understanding and serve no productive purpose in advancing their cause. I can't suggest reading *The Tao of Physics* or *The Self-Aware Universe* indiscriminately. Even *The Nag Hammadi Library* volume is useless without prerequisite study having been done."

"You've jumped to the extreme," she informed. "You could suggest *The Gnostic Gospels* by Elaine Pagels. That one isn't nearly as technical as the others and would be understood by most readers. It's also a small book."

"Well, yes."

"Mary, new agers confine themselves into a metaphysical box. They tend to hamper their development by never giving a single thought to intellectual expansion through researching and exploring the broader, related realities. How about suggesting *The Golden Bough* as reading material?"

"Mmmm," I hedged, "that's a big volume. Though it's a philosophical classic, the very size of it may put people off. I think your idea of Pagels' book was good. I'll have to give your idea more thought."

That was good enough for her. "There're some great works available out there that are being overlooked."

"Great. Yes . . . ."

"What," she asked, sensing a new aspect was about to enter our discourse.

"You said 'great works,' and that led me elsewhere. We recognize great works through their distinction of becoming classics, but . . . ."

"Your works will be classics one day," she slipped in, "it's a given. *Spirit Song* came out in 1985 and it's still outselling all your others."

Ignoring her statement, I continued my train of thought. "But how are 'great' *people* determined? By what criteria is greatness determined?"

"Accomplishments. Excelling in sport. Edison. Mother Teresa. Tesla and Shakespeare. William Blake." Her hand came up in a halting sign. "Now, I'm not agreeing that these qualities and people represent true greatness. Accomplishments and contributions are the criteria *society* uses to determine greatness. I mean, is Einstein great?"

"He could've been. He certainly had the potential for that distinction, but not when he urged Franklin Roosevelt to get into the business of nuclear fission."

"Many would disagree with that. Einstein let Roosevelt know that Germany was experimenting with nuclear fission. The Manhattan Project was seen by many to skyrocket the U.S. into the enviable position of military superiority."

"*Enviable* position? Look, we're getting away from the issue of greatness. Yes, I'm sure society as a whole views the man as great, but what I'm focusing on is not the guidelines society determines greatness by, but rather the criteria by which God qualifies greatness. Society's criteria are skewed. Subjective relativism plays a heavy hand in society's perspective; however, God's criteria aren't open to such fickle variances of human opinion."

"You're talking about this quality as perceived by God rather than as seen from a human world view."

"Yes, that's the only kind that holds spiritual worth. God sees greatness in the many, while humankind reveres the few to elevate to such public status."

"You've just reminded me of a parable you wrote in *Whispered Wisdom* about accomplishment, something about making one's *entire* life an accomplishment instead of accomplishing *one* deed in one's life. This is about that, isn't it."

"That and more. I also wrote about God being the *only* one we need to please in life. When we live our lives according to spiritual guidelines, we achieve greatness in God's eyes. When we routinely practice unconditional goodness, and make little sacrifices for others, we are seen as great by the Creator. Thus do we stand out as the living lights of earth, who brightly shine as beacons up into the heavens.

"True greatness is not being the star football player or the scientist making the breakthrough discovery. It's not the Shakespeares or Madame Curies of the world. True greatness may be found in the embodiment of the garbage man, store clerk, or neighbor. It may be found in the face that reflects in one's own mirror. Greatness grows brighter through the daily living and practical application of spiritual qualities and attributes. In word and deed, greatness blossoms forth as an everblooming flower, the fragrance being a pleasing incense honoring God. When one makes his or her entire life a song of the spirit, that person's life becomes a sweet and sacred hymn that God hears rising above all other sounds. It rises clear and true above the collective din of earth. These ones have true greatness.

"What's sad to me is that so many people have this 'singular mind-set' in regard to accomplishment. My correspondence underscores this widespread belief, when letter after letter cries out to know 'purpose' in life. People identify 'purpose' as being a single event or goal when, ninety-nine times out of one hundred, it's so much more than that because it's *how* one lives *daily* life. It's the *silent* greatness in us that lights us up and burns within us as a gentle votive candle flame upon our soul's altar. That is true greatness. When that is seen as a 'purpose' in life . . . that is greatness. Living to please God and God alone . . . that is greatness, for what other purpose are we here for?"

"People see purpose as *being* someone; someone recognized by others. Maybe a healer, shamanness, or teacher is what they have in mind," Sally said.

"I see that in my correspondence. That's ego. I cringe when I hear someone say, 'I've been told I'm to be a healer or shamanness, but I don't know anything about it or how to be one.' What? They were *told*? By whom? Who tells another what they must be? That's pure ego feeding another's thirsty ego!"

"Well?" Sally commented. "People feel purpose means being somebody, somebody who stands out from the others. Recognition. A specific skill. Unique."

"We're *all* unique! Every person on this planet is unique unto themselves and in their personal relationship with God. And 'purpose' is a *spiritual* ideal, not a corporeal one."

"That's not how people see it. It's not enough because . . . ."

"Not enough? Not enough! It's not *enough* to live a life that pleases *God*?"

"They need to please self, their ego of self first. Self-gratification."

I sighed. "True greatness will never be theirs. They are all here for the purpose of living a life that is pleasing to God. That's the singular answer to the age-old question. There is none other."

I sipped on the tea. "This is good."

"Thought you'd enjoy something different. You usually alternate your drinks as the evening wears on. Oh," she exclaimed, "I forgot to tell you, Preston said he's changing the name of his restaurant to *Fusion Grill*."

"How come?"

She shrugged. "I think he wants a change but the menu's still going to be as good as ever."

"That's the best place to eat in Woodland Park. That's where I did a lot of my early writing, you know, back when it was Godmother's Kitchen."

She nodded. "I know. What've you heard of the former owners?"

"They moved down south of Pueblo. Their son delivered us the cordwood. He and his friend are the ones you gave the work gloves to."

"Small world."

"You can say that again."

"Small world."

"Smart-mouth," I grinned, before releasing a relaxed sigh.

∞ ∞ ∞

"This is so nice sitting here like this," I whispered. "The crackling fire, warm glow on the walls, and sleeping dogs snuggled about the room. You can't buy this kind of peacefulness."

"The peacefulness doesn't come from these things, though," she said. "They only accentuate and heighten the peacefulness that exists within the self. Without that, the woodfire could crackle and snap till doomsday and it wouldn't have a peaceful effect. You're in a good place, Mary. And I don't mean physically—here in this cabin, I mean where you're at mentally and emotionally. You were dragged through a lot of darkness for a time and you pulled yourself out into the sunlight. You're in a good place."

I stared into the fire. "Yes, a good place. A place of lightness. Though my feet are firmly set upon the ground, I also feel as though a great anchor has been cut free of my heart and spirit. I have a certain buoyancy I never had before." I looked to my friend and grimaced. "Maybe I'm not explaining myself very well because that sounded a bit corny to me."

"You got the idea across just the same."

I looked off into the illumination of the silver valley and became pensive then.

Sally had become accustomed to my frequent moments of deep thought that appeared to distance me from my immediate surroundings. There were varied causal factors for these. I could be processing a mental visual—vision—that suddenly presented itself on the screen of my consciousness; I could be receiving an inspirational thought or conceptual idea from a variety of sources; or, I could have slipped into one of my own contemplative states that carried me deep into philosophical complexity. My friend respected this special moment and patiently waited for me to return my attention to the present.

I was aware of her softly whispering to Baby in a soothing tone. Her voice sounded as though it were coming from a great distance, almost from another dimension. Gradually, it became clearer and more distinct.

Finally, I turned to her. "Sorry for the interruption," I said.

"No problem."

"I know, yet I feel I'm being rude when that happens. I mean . . . I just *leave* all of a sudden."

"Hey, that's how it is being around you. It's your natural way. One gets used to it. Don't apologize for being you."

"Consciousness is an enigma," I said. "It's an enigma for people to understand."

Sally didn't respond, rather opting to let me carry out my thoughts.

"I recently read a book written by a neuroscientist. She wrote about how difficult it was to pin down a definitive definition for consciousness. It was clear that, throughout her book, her main problematical error was considering consciousness to be either a state of 'awake' awareness or some form of 'asleep' state of unconsciousness. By basing her entire idea of consciousness on this narrow premise, she narrowly confined the issue to one entirely dependent on the electrical machinations of the physical brain. Know what I'm saying?"

A nod of the head encouraged me to continue.

"Consciousness evidences the life of the spirit. It is mind that is not dependent on a mechanized brain for its existence. This is proven out when the consciousness is 'active' in the dream state that, on the surface, *appears* to be a state where we are physically unconscious. It is proven out when we experience afterlife following the death of the mechanized brain function. And consciousness is active while a coma state is in progress; here it is active on another dimensional level. In *quantum* meditation, consciousness journeys elsewhere and experiences vivid *virtual* events that are just as real as those experienced in the awake state.

"Consciousness is mind, not brain matter. Consciousness is spirit. The whole of our consciousness encompasses the totality of all the experiential personalities our spirit has ever manifested within. The whole of our consciousness retains all memory of same. Consciousness is energy, able to function as an intelligent force that carries the potentiality of boundless, unrestricted movement. Our consciousness is timeless, in that it transcends such insubstantial delineation as time. Therefore, consciousness is capable of containing our current life past, present, and future selves in a simultaneous, static state."

Now a frown came from across the room.

"Rephrase that last statement, please."

"Within your consciousness exists Sally as a child, Sally today, and Sally as an older person: past, present, and future consciousness aspects of the *current* Sally. This is so because time has no hold on consciousness. See?"

She did. "It explains how one can view the past, have cognition of different locales today, and know the future, too."

"Yes. And this also explains why I've had the clear impression of seeing the Elder of myself in the mirror sometimes. It explains how my Child Within can remain within the static consciousness of an eternal six year old."

Sally expressed concern. "Society believes that these aspects of one's consciousness are the so-called 'split personalities.'"

"Society is wrong about these specific, natural aspects. Society, as has been proven by the writings of various neuroscientists, does not yet have a clear comprehension of consciousness. It doesn't know what to make of it, nor can it imagine its vast potentialities."

My friend's voice was questioning with reservation. "Why do I have the feeling that you're thinking of addressing this in one of your future books?"

"You're psychic?"

"Get serious." Then her mouth dropped. "Oh Lord, you *are* serious!"

I said nothing.

"Are you going to expose Little Self to the world?"

"It's time."

"But, Mary, you've not mentioned her to anyone. I'm the only living person she's revealed herself to."

"That's because, as she explained, you were the only person she trusted. Until that night back at the stone cabin, when she came forward and talked directly to you, I myself had no idea she even existed as a past, living aspect of my current consciousness." I smiled then. "No wonder I always collected children's books for myself . . . they were, in reality, for Little Self—my Child Within."

"Ohhh, I don't know about this, Mary."

"You're afraid of how such knowledge will be received by the public, but I believe the reality of consciousness needs to be explained in a living manner. Little Self spoke to you, told you personal things, detailed how so many of our past lives were closely related and clarified why you felt so drawn to being my helper and companion. This was why you came—your spirit's purpose. It was Little Self who brought all the loose ends together with the facts."

Sally smiled with the remembrance. "She was so precocious! So animated and cute. I was blown away by how intelligent and knowledgeable she was of the spirit plane and the technicalities of true reality. She seemed to be a well of information."

"That's because she maintains a bidimensional consciousness—one that easily spans the Here and the There. Same with the Elder within me. She's 94." I chuckled with speculation. "I wonder if that means I'm going to live to be that age. Do you think?"

Sally sighed. "Wouldn't that be a 'probability' potentiality if nothing changes to alter that future self of your consciousness?"

"That's what I think, too."

"Mary . . . are you seriously thinking about revealing these aspects of you?"

"You already asked me that. The issue of consciousness is too much of a mystery to even the scientists. What then can the average Jane Doe understand of it if someone doesn't attempt to clarify it?

"I've been thinking a great deal on this subject," I said. "I'm going to do a book dealing with consciousness *speculation*. I think it will be my next work."

"Oh, God."

"What?" I asked, "you don't think it's a good idea?"

"It's a little scary, that's all."

"Not if it's 'speculation' . . . theoretical, in a sense."

"Oh, sure, theoretical on the surface, but overflowing with facts."

"Yes."

"I don't know about this."

"I do. I'm going to do it. I'm going ahead with it. I already have a title."

"Well then I guess you have been giving this a lot of thought. What's the title?"

"*Keeper of the Soul.*"

She thought on that. "I like that, I like it a lot. The *Keeper* is Little Self, isn't she."

"Yes. She's watched over me all my life . . . keeping hurtful incidents of my childhood to herself, watching and guiding in her own quiet way. She's been my keeper for a long time."

"Do you think she's going to object to exposing her?"

"She's excited about this. She wants to be a part of helping people understand their own consciousness and the reality of its various living aspects." Sally caught the sudden glint in my eye. "Maybe she'll tell you that the next time she talks to you."

"She said she'd do that again sometime, but she's been quiet since we moved here."

"If she said she'd talk to you again, she will. It's up to her."

"Sometimes I catch a glimpse of her in you. Some of your mannerisms make me think she's real close to the surface."

I didn't comment.

Sally was thoughtful.

Changing the subject, I said. "In one of the letters I received yesterday, the lady wanted to know why

I didn't have a Web site like other authors do. She asked me for my e-mail address."

"That'd be a good trick without electricity in the cabin."

"Well, yes, but . . . is everything becoming high-tech electronics out there now?"

"Becoming? It already is!"

"Not for me, it isn't."

"No, I don't believe it will ever be that for you. Having a basic phone and a fax machine is as technical as you'll ever get, isn't it."

I nodded. "I don't see it as being left behind, either. I see it as a choice to stay out of the loop that will one day become a snare. Besides, all that electronic correspondence is so impersonal. It's not private, either. I'd much rather correspond the old-fashioned way with letters and hand-written cards. If it weren't for the business of my writing, I wouldn't even have that fax machine." I frowned. "Can't figure that thing out half the time . . . it's got too many whistles and buttons! I live in a fast-developing electronic age, yet have no desire for any of it."

"I think what your correspondent really wants to know is why you're not making yourself more accessible like other authors do."

"That's a form of PR, isn't it? It's a way of keeping oneself before the public eye–consciousness–staying current and being 'what's happening.'" Shrugging off the idea, I said, "Maintaining oneself as a 'current fad' or the 'woman of the moment' status isn't why I'm here. Once I've communicated all the messages and concepts I've come to give, then my work is done. The light at the end of the tunnel has already shown itself."

She in no way shared my excitement. "You're needed on this planet whether you've said all you came to say or not. Don't you see that? Whether you're writing books or not, your presence here makes a difference. How many readers have told you that? Huh?"

"We all make a difference, Sally. Every single one of us makes a vibratory ripple upon the Web's fine strands of life. As we live and breathe we try to generously uplift those around us while appreciating life's incredible beauty and blessings. Living life through behavior that pleases God makes for a glorified life full of grace and light. It's the treasure one takes into the Great Beyond and lays before the feet of God."

"There's a zillion of your readers out there who would dearly love to see you hold onto your 'treasure' till you're at least a hundred years old. Your readers . . . ."

The hair on my scalp stood on end as I watched her eyes suddenly round to saucers and her jaw fall open. She stared past me out the picture window.

"M-m-mary," she murmured, while creeping across the room toward the window. "What the hell is *out* there?"

I leaned forward in my chair and looked out into the moonlit valley. I frowned as a chilling ripple coursed down my spine. I climbed onto the cedar chest for a better view.

Now we were shoulder to shoulder.

Eyes riveted to three floating orbs of bright light, we watched the two smaller ones, which were about the size of a hubcap, circle and dance around the larger one, which was like a huge beachball.

Around and over they glided.

Flitting like magnified fairy light.

"What are they?" Sally asked without daring to take her eyes from the amazing sight. "They're right *there*!"

She got that right. They were right there, right smack dab in front of the cabin.

"They remind me of the ball of light I nearly touched as it flew over me the night that military helicopter chased it. These are like that."

"Starborn stuff," she whispered.

"Maybe."

"Maybe? Oh!" she exclaimed, "look how they're moving around! They're so bright!"

"Sally?"

"What?"

"The dogs aren't barking."

She took a millisecond to take her eyes off the valley to check behind us. Wide eyes then met mine. "They're sleeping!"

Goosebumps rippled down my arms. "Maybe these lights are what they've been charging around at all evening. Maybe they've been coming and going around the cabin and we just couldn't see them, but the dogs sensed them."

"Think so?"

I shrugged with uncertainty. "Sounds plausible."

"So why aren't they sensing them now?"

"Now they're not supposed to," I replied. "Now is for us."

We watched the large ball of light float around the silvery valley while the two smaller orbs continued to dance about it. We watched for about twelve minutes. Then they vanished like extinguished candle flames.

We looked at one another.

"It's late and I'm tired," I announced. "I need to go to bed. You going to stay up and paint?"

She glanced out at the empty valley. "Not tonight. I'll let the dogs out one last time."

"I'll close up the woodstove and turn the generator off."

Baby followed Sally up into her bedroom.

The rest of the little people followed on my heels into my room. Cheyenne crawled under the bed and Pinecone, Rosie and Punkin settled in their favorite spots around me.

The oil pot burned with a steady flame on my dresser. It reflected warmly over the knotty pine. It was a room of deep comfort for me. It represented a great deal of hard work. This was a good place. Despite having no electricity and needing a lot more construction work, it was a good place.

"Mary?" came a voice from across the hall.

"What?" I called back.

"I don't want a skylight over my bed, either."

"Goodnight, Sally."

"You think so?"

"Do I think what?"

"That we'll have a good night . . . a quiet night."

"You on good terms with your guardian angel?"

"Well . . . yeah, I guess so."

"Then goodnight, Sally."

I fell asleep thinking how wonderful it was that we had one less house project to work on.

No skylights.

Books by Mary Summer Rain

Since 1985, when **Spirit Song** *first appeared, uncounted thousands have discovered Mary Summer Rain and "No-Eyes," the wise old Native American woman who taught the young Mary Summer Rain many things. The following books have been written and published:*

Spirit Song: The Visionary Wisdom of No-Eyes (1985), relates how the two first met. Although totally blind from birth, No-Eyes lived on the land, identifying everything she needed by smell and touch. Using gentle discipline, humor, and insight, she guided Summer Rain through a remarkable series of experiences, giving her the accumulated knowledge of her own eight decades.

Phoenix Rising: No-Eyes' Vision of the Changes to Come (1987), used the analogy of the phoenix, the mythical bird that symbolizes rebirth and eternal life, to provide a powerful warning of the earth changes in store for us. This unforgettable prophecy has already begun to come true, as the daily newspaper and TV news broadcasts demonstrate.

Dreamwalker: The Path of Sacred Power (1988), is the story of No-Eyes' introduction of Mary to Brian Many Heart, who taught Mary the power of the Dreamwalker by bringing her to face some painful realities. In it, she deals with many unanswered questions about her own identity and her role in traveling the path of knowledge. One of the best spirit-walking books in print.

Phantoms Afoot: Journeys Into the Night (1989), is a fascinating description of the quiet work done by Mary and her husband Bill in liberating spirits lost between two worlds. You might call these ghost stories, but ghost stories told with concern for the welfare of the ghost! Like the previous three volumes, *Phantoms Afoot* is very much set in Colorado. All the wild beauty of the Colorado countryside enters into the story.

Earthway (1990), Mary Summer Rain's fifth book, is a presentation of the knowledge of the Native Americans. Interweaving the inspired teachings of No-Eyes with a wealth of practical knowledge of all kinds, she demonstrated a practical, gentle, *civilized* way of life. Divided into sections for body, mind and spirit, the book aimed at restoring wholeness. (Published by Pocket Books, but available from Hampton Roads.)

Daybreak: The Dawning Ember (1991), Mary's sixth book, is divided into two parts. "The Communion" consisted of extensive answers to questions she had received from readers over the years. Ranging from prophecy to Native American history, from metaphysics to just plain common sense, here were nearly 450 pages of wisdom, including an extensive section on dream interpretation.

The second section, called "The Phoenix Files," is a comprehensive collection of maps, charts, lists, and tables describing nuclear facilities, toxic-waste dumps, oil refineries, hurricane, tornado and flood-hazard zones, as well as a suggested pole-shift realignment configuration. Together, it made an indispensable resource manual.

Soul Sounds: Mourning the Tears of Truth (1992), is the book Mary's readers long waited for: her own story, in her own words, of the experiences that shaped her extraordinary life, from childhood to her most recent meetings with Starborn friends. This was her private journal, written for herself and for her children. She didn't want it published. But her advisors insisted, and finally she gave in. . .and the reader reaction has been nothing short of phenomenal.

Mountains, Meadows and Moonbeams: A Child's Spiritual Reader (1984, 1992), was originally privately printed by Mary and Bill. Only in 1992 was the first trade paperback edition made available by Hampton Roads Publishing Company. This simple, delightful, easy-to-read book is full of illustrations for coloring; it will help parents nurture the creativity and imagination of their children; and will help children to understand where we come from and who we as humans really are.

Whispered Wisdom (1993) is a collection of beautiful photographs taken by Mary Summer Rain which depict the four seasons of Colorado. It is a celebration of nature, accompanied by a collection of verse, prose, vignettes, and sayings taken from her woods-walking journal. Together the pictures and words weave a wonderful tapestry of the many faces of Mother Earth.

Ancient Echoes (1993) is a magical collection of chants, prayers, and songs of the Anasazi people, who lived in pueblos on the plateau area of the American Southwest from around 100 to 1300 A.D. Mary Summer Rain brings forth the beauty and sensitivity of the Anasazi heart by recreating many of the chants used by one Anasazi community called the Spirit Clan. The information came from "spiritual memory recall," whereby she received, in deep meditative states, both the words and the spirit of the words. These chants, prayers, and songs also have many practical uses, for healing, blessings, child sleep songs, for a broken heart. Illustrated with line drawings, it is a stunning and practical book.

The Seventh Mesa (1994) is Mary Summer Rain's first novel, though she pointedly asks the question for the reader to decide: is it *really* fiction? It's about a hidden pyramid buried beneath a Southwest mesa, and a guarded chamber that holds the sacred scrolls and tablets which reveal the answers to humanity's most puzzling mysteries through the ages. But is it time for us to discover those answers? Have we gained enough wisdom to know what to do with that information? Four interesting characters come together to take that fascinating and dangerous adventure.

Bittersweet (1995) is a continuation of the *Soul Sounds* journal, but in the format of a collection of stories, rather than a day-by-day diary. It deals with the outstanding events in Mary Summer Rain's life since 1992. Some of these events, including her interactions with her Starborn friend, are quite astounding in their implications. Illustrated with line drawings, and a twelve-page color photo section, *Bittersweet* will be one of the most informative, interesting, and controversial books for Mary Summer Rain's readers.

Mary Summer Rain's Guide to Dream Symbols (1996) with Alex Greystone. For years readers have written Mary Summer Rain requesting interpretations of literally hundreds of their dreams. In both *Earthway* and *Daybreak*, she addressed this need, adding a short list of interpreted dream symbols. Here, in collaboration with Alex Greystone, she has created an entirely new, single-volume reference guide to more than 14,500 dream symbols. *Mary Summer Rain on Dreams* is a comprehensive dictionary of dream symbols and "key word" clues, with short, succinct, easy-to-understand interpretations. She has shared her insight into the world of spirit, giving us a powerful interpretive tool to help in our own transformative journeys.

The Visitation: An Archangel's Prophecy (1997). In a vivid dream in June 1996, Mary Summer Rain had a visitation. "I was sitting in my reading chair, and the room began growing brighter and brighter until a radiant being appeared." He had shoulder-length blond hair and electric blue eyes, and she sensed that he was an archangel. He gave what amounts to an address on the "state of the human soul," the prophetic consequences of humanity's present course of action "as time marches on toward Armageddon." This discourse is our wake-up call, a plea to stop the precipitous slide toward disaster for ourselves, our planet, our children—before it's too late. The Visitation may be Mary Summer Rain's most powerful message to the world.

Star Babies (1997). Few children's books convey the message that we are not alone in the universe. Mary Summer Rain, who has had contact with the "Starborns" for many years, dedicates *Star Babies* ". . . to the new and enlightened generation of children who will foster the understanding that our true reality is a vast universe peopled with God's children, that we are all intelligent human beings sharing one Universe, one neighborhood, and that there is no such thing as an alien." It is Mary's hope that this generation of children will pave the way for first contact, but they must be shown that there is nothing to fear from our neighbors in the stars.

Millennium Memories (1997). This Millennium ends on the last day of the year 2000. The period from 1998 through 2000 is considered by prophets from Nostradamus to Edgar Cayce as one of the most important in human history. It's predicted to be a time of great change—physical, mental, and spiritual—for the Earth and all its inhabitants. Since mind is the builder, what we focus on is what we will create in the years ahead. Here Mary Summer Rain, who has been keeping a daily journal for years, shares the wisdom and the wonder of the journaling experience with her readers. She has created a day-by-day journal for this three-year period, filled with inspirational wisdom, encouraging people to keep a daily record of their lives. By focusing on the positive and maintaining a spiritual perspective, we can all see our way through the difficult times ahead to the birth of a new world.